DISCIPLINE *with* *LOVE*

Legends in Dog Training

KURT THOMAS WOLFF

ISBN 979-8-89428-767-6 (paperback)
ISBN 979-8-89637-179-3 (hardcover)
ISBN 979-8-89428-768-3 (digital)

Christian Faith Publishing
832 Park Avenue
Meadville, PA 16335
www.christianfaithpublishing.com

Printed in the United States of America

A Dog's Prayer

Whisper my name as I surround you.
Remembering my earthly years of love
allows my soul to walk by your side forever.

Contents

Special Acknowledgments

CAPTAIN ARTHUR HAGGERTY, my mentor in becoming a professional dog trainer.

Flo Bosie, assistant dog training instructor.

Sal Limoli, who gave me the idea and inspiration to become a dog trainer.

Sharon Hubbard, an editor of a local paper who helped edit and give professional advice.

Laura Bonavia, who assisted in the typing and editing of this book.

Michele Mark, my niece who worked with me in my early years, inspiring me to never give up.

Introduction

YOU ARE ABOUT to read true stories about my unique adventures during the past forty years as a professional dog trainer. Many of you may relate to the stories and understand my presentation of the human-dog relationships.

Therefore, let me take you on my journey of a lifetime, featuring captured moments.

This book is dedicated to all my friends, relatives, clients, fellow dog lovers, and especially my wonderful wife, who dedicated herself by helping me to write the stories.

Discipline with Love
(Birth of a Dog)

MANKIND HAS PROVEN through many years of DNA research that our beloved friend is closely related to the wolf. Personally, I believe there is a much simpler explanation. The Bible states that Adam and Eve were the first humans to arrive on planet Earth. Behaviorists claim that a dog is man's best friend, so it's obvious the dog had to arrive sometime after Adam and Eve. Don't question me on how I know; it's just the way I see it logically and as a sound conclusion. Many of us are familiar with the biblical story of Adam and Eve. They had children, and both Adam and Eve went on to live long lives.

"On a chilled moonlit night, Adam decided to ask God for a new friend. He complained that his children were all grown and no longer lived at home and that his wife's affection has somehow diminished from what it once was. Too old for a new wife, the Lord delivered his new arrival. A wonderful bundle of fur graciously licked Adam relentlessly. A merry event of happiness transcended onto Adam, who said, 'Thank you, Lord. Thank you! What do I call this magnificent entity, which loves me with so much passion?' The Lord answered, 'Spell my name backwards, Adam, and you shall reveal his given name, dog! Also, remember to use discipline with love, and he will be your friend forever!'"

This story may or may not be the true genesis of our dog, but what we are certain of is that the dog is truly a gift bestowed on all of mankind. Therefore, it is my obligation to help all dog owners to learn how to train and respect their new friend by using discipline with love!

Like my story of Adam, if you also experience a special dog in your life, words alone could never express this deep emotional feeling. You, like Adam, have experienced this gift: dog! Unfortunately, some people misunderstand their dogs, and they never quite accomplish a loving human-canine relationship. Before I proceed any further, please understand that your dog is not human! *Webster's* definition of *anthropomorphism* is that it is an interpretation of which is not human or personal in terms of human or personal characteristics— humanization. A dog is just being a dog when he or she jumps, barks, chews, and displays antics that are clearly misunderstood by human beings. It is my sole purpose to educate you, in dog psychology, why your dog does what he or she does and communicates in a similar expression in which dogs transmit to each other! Hitting stems from a human emotion used out of frustration with the intent to hurt or punish. Dogs never hit each other while living in a pack, and there- fore this gesture, when used by a human, will trigger fight or flight! A threat to your dog by you will be detrimental in obtaining future positive communications. A dog will only trust, obey, and bond with you when a training method is focused on his or her mental capacity. Genetics and early environmental experiences play a future role in a dog's life. As a human, it's important to interpret why a dog partic- ipates in behaviors that are undesirable to you and to control these behaviors by using a training method of communication by which a dog is genetically programmed to understand! When all is said and done, your dog will go from being a spoiled trained dog to a trained spoiled dog. After all, what's the sense of having a dog you can't spoil? Your dog will get off the couch and lie down in his or her own bed when you learn to use discipline with love.

Like Adam, if you have ever owned and bonded with a special dog in your life, you know that words alone could never express this deep emotional feeling. You are one among the few who experience this gift. Unfortunately, not all dog owners receive or even under- stand this unique bond of human-dog relationship. Many people, in their untimely rush, end up with a dog that is out of control and therefore difficult to train. Untimely human emotions could result from not being able to effectively communicate with their newly acquired puppy or dog. The fact is that many of these canine friends end up being returned to the breeder, previous owner, or shelter.

Prevention:

Of course, the worst end may be euthanizing; leaving the house to run off; selling to dog fighting rings, the dog trade, laboratories; or many other inhumane ends.

Reward:

If you love your dog and respect him or her enough to learn to communicate, then I will promise you that this book will cover all the communication necessary for you to learn discipline with love. Interacting through training, playing, and communication with your best friend will undoubtedly reward you with unconditional love.

TV Time

THIS WAS MY day to be on television for the first time. I had sold a trained dog to a television consumer reporter at channel 12, located in Long Island, New York. She asked if I would be interested in doing a short demonstration at the famous Bide-A-Wee shelter, which would tremendously help in getting dogs adopted. I told her that it was an honor for me to be chosen to do this. After all, not only was I helping dogs to be adopted; it was also an excellent way to promote my dog training school. My only concern was that I didn't want to interfere with, take away from, step on the toes of, or pull rank on the dog trainer that helped out at this shelter.

The television reporter reassured me that she wanted me for this shelter dog promo, not the other dog trainer. Upon our arrival, we were greeted by the manager of the Bide-A-Wee shelter. I could sense right from the start that this manager was not too pleased about me being the selected dog trainer! This resentment was soon to be highlighted when he selected the dog for me to leash up. My experience as a professional dog trainer was soon challenged by a hyperactive female German shepherd. Keep in mind that when a dog is being released from a confined area, the anticipation of freedom can be an overwhelming event. This high-powered young German shepherd attempted to drag me all over the outside parking lot. One thing that I was confident in knowing was that this dog, along with all the people watching, were about to witness the transition from a crazed dog to a disciplined dog, or my name wasn't Kurt Wolff.

Believe it when I say that the pressure was on me! Here I was, camera rolling, people watching, and during this demonstration, I was being recorded in real time. I was always confident, knowing that my method was excellent, and this was the time to prove it to the public.

Normally, it would only take two or three minutes for me to gain control over a dog in the heel command. However, this shepherd girl was like a released tiger kept in captivity for years. The only plus was that she was a nonaggressive tiger! A hyperaggressive dog would have been the ultimate challenge. This dog was a strong, hyperactive young dog who had been cooped up in a small kennel and most likely never had any previous training. Being locked up in a kennel was a significant factor in her behavior, and I didn't have any idea of how long she had been enclosed. Her actions proved that she was oblivious to the present environment. It took me fifteen minutes to gain some decent control in the heel command, which would normally have taken me only two or three minutes. It took another ten minutes to finally get her to sit-stay with the news reporter as she shouted out about the dog shelter. My pure determination allowed for a wonderful presentation of the German shepherd sitting alongside the persistent newscaster. Believe me that this wasn't an easy accomplishment.

After the outside taping, we entered the shelter for an interview with the Bide-A-Wee manager. He was asked numerous questions on shelter operation and the placing of dogs into new homes. When asked about the German shepherd I had just trained, he said, "Oh, that dog has had previous obedience training!" Knowing that discretion was the better part of valor was the only reason I didn't attack his statement. If that dog had any formal training, it must have been in her previous life. Having received that insult wasn't too hard to understand as I had taken the play from him and his shelter dog trainer. Also, if the trainer was the one supposedly trained her, then it was time for him to seek another occupation. The big plus was that the German shepherd girl was soon adopted after she was seen on television. I would be more than happy to do it all again, just knowing that a dog would be released from this shelter into a caring home and, most of all, loved.

Key notes on behavior training:

In this case, we have a situation where a dog is cooped up for a period of time. The length of time in which the dog is confined can contribute to the behavioral circumstances at hand. Another factor would be the dog's history prior to being sheltered. In many cases, the truth is not always told. I am a firm believer that early environment has most to do with the outcome of a dog's personality. The majority of dogs can be helped tremendously when trained properly using discipline with love. Teaching the heel command will give you 75 percent of the necessary control in order to be successful in communicating. This German shepherd girl was a great example.

Sal and Sam (Birth of My Dog Training Career)

LATE IN THE winter of 1971, my dream of becoming a professional dog trainer finally became a reality. My lifelong friend Sal was instrumental in making this dream come true. Sal and I played basketball together during our teenage years and into the better part of our early adult life. We were fortunate to have the use of a basketball court on Wednesday nights at a local grade school on Long Island, New York. Sal was always thinking of ways to make extra money, and a week prior to this evening, he showed me a stuffed mechanical dog named Lucky, which would walk and bark when you called it. On this particular Wednesday night, while in the locker room, after a couple of hours of basketball, Sal informed me that he had a special dog to show me. I couldn't imagine what other kind of mechanical dog he was going to show me out in the parking lot of the school.

On that memorable night in 1971, Sal opened his car door, and out jumped a black Labrador mix named Sam. Sal had rescued this dog from a local shelter and already had some basic control over Sam. He demonstrated the commands heel, sit, stay, down, and come when called. After the demonstration, Sal commanded Sam to jump back into his car. I was very impressed and, I must say, a bit jealous. When I asked who trained the dog for him, Sal informed me that he went to the library and checked out a book called *Training You to Train Your Dog*, written by Blanche Saunders. He had trained Sam by reading Saunder's book.

We then both drove off in separate cars to a nearby restaurant we frequented every Wednesday after playing basketball. It was during that drive to the restaurant that I envisioned myself as a professional dog trainer. I knew, if Sal could train a dog, there was no reason why I couldn't do the same. There was absolutely no doubt in my mind that I was to be a dog trainer! During dinner, I told Sal that I was going to be a dog trainer and that he should also consider the profession.

I suggested that we research the profession by locating a professional dog training school in order to learn all the necessary methods to become qualified dog trainers. Sal agreed to help me locate a reputable dog training school. We went to a couple of schools, which were highly recommended. But although the owners seemed to be well-spoken and knowledgeable on the subject of dog training, the interviews turned out to be disappointing. While visiting one training school, the owner was sitting behind his desk while Sal and I sat opposite him. The door to the office flew open, and in ran a cute puppy. He grabbed the pup by the crest of his neck and flung him across the floor toward an employee. Here was a renowned dog trainer, displaying a raging anger toward an innocent puppy, not to mention he displayed this rage in front of two potential students. We left abruptly. After this incident, Sal decided he did not want to pursue the profession, but I wasn't going to let this unkind act offset my desire to try and locate someone who could teach me the dog training profession.

Finally, the break came when I was referred to Captain Haggerty's School for Dogs. I called, set up an appointment, and drove off to the South Bronx. I met with the owner, Captain Arthur Haggerty. After a few minutes of my interviewing Captain Haggerty, I knew that this intelligent gentleman was going to be the one to teach me the dog training profession. It was May 1971, and in six months after completing the dog training course, I received my diploma. Now I was a certified professional behaviorist dog trainer!

My humble gratitude goes to my friend Sal, Captain Haggerty, and Flo, the dog training school's assistant instructor. All gave me the vision and knowledge to become who I am today, a man with direction, as I walk this earth with meaning and purpose, training dogs and their owners using discipline with love!

My Duke

THE DESIRE TO own a dog started sometime in 1970. I was working for Pan American airlines and had known for some time that they would be going out of business.

When I decided to become a dog trainer, I read a few dog training books and quickly realized that in order to learn this profession, I would have to locate a renowned dog training school. Therefore, I needed a dog to practice with as I acquired dog training skills. A coworker at Pan Am informed me that his parents had a German shepherd that they wanted to sell. His parents had purchased Duke while on vacation in Pennsylvania. They spent the entire summer with Duke before returning back home to Brooklyn. During that summer, he was always with a member of the family. When the family went back to work, Duke was left alone, resulting in separation anxiety. After all, this was his first experience of being left isolated. Duke's separation anxiety created a bad case of destructive chewing!

When I purchased Duke, Tommy and his parents told me how sweet and gentle he is. They somehow neglected to inform me of Duke's separation anxiety! They said they just didn't have enough time to spend with him since they have to work every day. I had no idea what was in store for me; after all, this event took place six months before I started the Captain Haggerty's dog training school.

One evening, my wife and I went out and later came back to find Duke had destroyed the inside of the house. If I had known about separation anxiety and the cause of this behavior, perhaps this could have been avoided. When I informed Tommy about Duke, he confessed to me about Duke destroying the apartment. He neglected to tell me, fearing that I wouldn't purchase Duke.

Prior to getting Duke, I constructed a dog run with a large dog house out, back in the yard. The dog kennel was constructed according to an air force military K-9 manual. The dog house was big enough to accommodate two large dogs. This was to be Duke's living quarters.

I started dog training school in May of 1971. Duke was an eager student, which enhanced the bond between us.

I lived on an acre of property that was filled with trees. When Duke was interested in sniffing something and not paying attention to me, I would sometimes step away from him, look for an easy tree to climb, and once up high enough, I would call, "Duke!" Of course this made locating me a little more difficult but that kept him focused on finding me. This hide-and-seek game trained Duke to be earnest in his quest, never to give up until he found me. When Duke found and joined up with me, he was rewarded with a treat. This game was immensely instrumental in gaining a positive come-when-called response. Hide-and-seek secured a tighter bond between us. I felt more secure hanging out with Duke off leash, knowing that he would never allow me out of his sight. Because of our strong bond, all our training lessons were enjoyable and easy for Duke to learn.

Once I felt secure that I had a trained dog, it was time to demonstrate him on consultations for obedience training.

One of the more memorable times was my first demonstration with Duke to show a potential client my dog training abilities. When I arrived for my consultation, I elected to leave Duke in my car until I was ready to demonstrate him. After I finished my introduction with the potential client, I informed them that I was going to my car to get Duke and demonstrate obedience. When I got out to my car, the interior of my two-year-old Volvo was destroyed. Pieces of the car seats, visors, and any other chewable material were scattered from the front to the back of the car. I still decided to take Duke into the home and demonstrate him in obedience. He gave a stellar performance, and I signed up the client for a six-week dog training program.

With Duke's help, my training skills improved. I knew, from this time on, that this profession would undoubtedly be a challenge! As a behaviorist dog trainer, I would have to understand clearly why dogs do what they do, and then intelligently solve their behavioral problems.

Prior to my owning Duke, he was studded out, and I acquired his daughter, Tonya, who soon became our newest member of the pack. This new addition was advantageous because I could teach adult obedience to Duke and puppy training to Tonya, which further increased my ability to educate dog owners in need of training.

We had many memorable days at the beach, lake, woods, park, and our yard. This reward was greatly enjoyable when both dogs are controlled off leash!

One day, I went to the kennel; I found Duke and Tonya were missing! Somehow, the kennel gate had sprung open. When I couldn't find them by driving around the neighborhood, I decided to call the local police and pound, but the authorities had no report on two German shepherds.

After a few hours, I just happened to be outside when Tonya came walking down the driveway toward the house. I asked Tonya, "Where is Duke?" Tonya began to whine and was noticeably upset! Later that day, at around 4:00 p.m., the Hempstead Town shelter called to inform me that they had picked up Duke and identified him by the ID tag on his safety collar, which had my name and phone number. They informed me that they were closing and that I could pick Duke up the following morning. I was upset that they called me too late to pick him up that day but felt relieved that Duke had been found and was safe.

When I arrived at the pound the following morning, I found Duke lying in a puddle of water. I frantically yelled his name! He tried desperately to get up but kept falling back down. When I approached the kennel to retrieve him, the pound officer abruptly instructed me to stay out! I was told that I wasn't authorized to enter any of the kennel runs and that I had to wait until the pound employees took him out! At the front office, I proceeded to sign all the necessary papers, pay the fine, and waited outside at the other end of the kennel run.

Two-pound officials tried to walk Duke out on a lead. Duke was slipping and falling due to a back injury that I was unaware of at the time. Once Duke was out of the run, I quickly ran over and grabbed the lead from one of the officials. After hugging and kissing him, I quickly picked Duke up and brought him over to the Wantagh Animal Hospital, which was conveniently located next door. The veterinarian at the hospital informed me that he had been called over to the pound when Duke arrived. A police officer told the vet that he believed Duke was hit by a car on the parkway. The vet said there were no signs of lacerations and therefore could wait till tomorrow. I said, "Why didn't you call me, after all his name and phone number was on the collar!"

He replied, "I probably should have called, but it was near closing time, and I elected to wait until the next day."

I left Duke, feeling that all was going to be okay while in veterinary care.

Later that day, I received the heartbreaking call that Duke had an injured back and had passed away! The vet admitted he was negligent in not closely examining Duke upon arrival and that perhaps Duke would have had stood a better chance of survival if he had taken the time to try and save him the day before. Even though the veterinarian apologized and admitted his wrongdoing, I believe that Duke became ill lying in a puddle of water all night!

I was totally torn apart inside, and all along I knew I had to stay strong. The Wantagh Bide-A-Wee animal cemetery is located close by the veterinary hospital; therefore, I decided to bury Duke there. His plot is approximately twenty feet away from a WWI dog hero, Sarge the war dog! On Duke's brass grave plaque is inscribed "DUKE ROLF OF DYBERRY, LOVED TO THE VERY END."

They say there is a positive side to every negative experience! I included the story of Duke here first, followed by many other dog-human experiences during my dog training career.

After each of the following profound stories, I learned from my mistakes, and there were many rewarding positive results to follow, especially now being able to share what I have learned with all dog owners.

Training notes:

First and foremost, research and know the history of any puppy or adult dog you purchase or adopt! Lack of this knowledge was ever so prevalent in the case of Duke. He had a tenacious separation problem called separation anxiety! As a puppy, he went from the security of his mother to the security of two human adults. Duke was never conditioned to be left alone! Lack of knowing this behavioral problem was soon to become a nightmare for Duke's owners. After vacation, Duke was soon to experience a drastic change in environmental surroundings. This young German shepherd puppy went from country freedom to being confined in a Brooklyn apartment. Consequently, Duke panicked when left alone! Dogs are pack animals and depend on the support of each other. This is especially essential during their puppy stage!

Second, secure your dog in a safe enclosure! My mistake was in not realizing that the latch on the gate was easily sprung open if hit or pushed upward. Duke opened the latch! A latch on any enclosure should be constructed to be dog proof—in other words, a latch that your dog can never spring open! In my case, if I had inserted a clip or lock in the hole of the latch, Duke would never have freed himself! All enclosures, whether cage, room, or kennel, should be carefully checked to make sure they are escape proof!

Also, check that your dog's collar can't get caught on any part of an enclosure! A flat collar with ID is the safest type of collar. ID tags that are riveted on will prevent tags from becoming hooked on any structure.

Finally, obedience train your puppy or adult dog! I can't stress enough the importance of owning an obedient dog and learning to communicate. It fosters a relationship of true love, security, and understanding. The basic commands of sit, down, stay, come, heel, and the correction word *no* are learned within the presentation of the training method and are immensely important. "Sit" and "stay" are instrumental in keeping your dog safe when the front door of your home is opened! "Heel" will give you 75 percent of the necessary control needed for your dog to respect and obey! If taught properly, the heel will also benefit the next learned command, come, when called. Your dog should come to you when called under any and all circumstances! If you love your dog, you will train him or her! A learned "no" will control all behavioral problems!

Experience, along with never-ending research, enabled me to learn and apply my skills in order to help other people and their dogs.

Thanks to Duke, I was determined to learn in earnest, to become who I am today, having loved helping our best friends and their families for the last forty years, and now to share what I have learned to help you and your best friend to communicate using my method of discipline with love.

Captured memories of Duke

At the lake. In the summer of 1971, I took Duke to my father-in-law's lake house in Pennsylvania for the weekend. Duke and I went to the lake, hoping he would swim out to retrieve a tennis ball but didn't have any luck getting him into the water. At this time, I was still attending Captain Haggerty's dog training school and asked Captain Haggerty how I could get Duke to swim in the lake. As he was teaching me how to use a method and connect it with behavior, he told me to figure it out on my own.

During this summer, my wife's father gave us permission to enjoy a week's vacation at the lake. We went with my dear friends Nick, Brigetta, and their two daughters, Terresa and Pam.

Fifty feet out on the lake was a floating dock. I swam out, stood on the dock, and yelled out to Duke, who was pacing back and forth on the shoreline. I remembered Captain Haggerty telling me to figure out for myself how to encourage Duke to swim. Facing the shoreline, I dived into the lake and swam under to the back side of the dock, where Duke could not see me. Then while hiding in the water, I began calling to him. I watched Duke pacing back and forth until finally he began to swim out to find me. Once he was halfway to the floating dock, I began to swim toward Duke, and we met halfway. I hugged him with tears, knowing that he was swimming out to find and save me.

Duke never hesitated to enter any body of water from that day on.

At the beach. In the fall of 1971, my wife, Janet, and I took Duke and his then four-month-old daughter, Tonya, to Jones Beach.

It was high tide, and there were many flooded pools of water for the dogs to run through. I took a few photographs of Duke and Tonya frolicking in the tide pools with the same beach and blue sky in the background.

Now that I knew Duke would not hesitate to swim, I tossed a rubber ball into the ocean. He swam out too far, trying to find the ball, and was engulfed in a wave. I was ready to dive in to save him, but he remembered his swimming lesson at the lake the summer before and managed to swim back out onto the beach. What a memorable day at the beach, and I still have the photographs to always remember the occasion.

At Mill Pond. In my first story about the birth of my dog training career, I wrote about my friend Sal and his mixed Labrador, Sam. Duke and Sam became great friends, and we all enjoyed outings together. One of these outings was at Mill Pond, a nearby lake and brook. At one end of the brook was a gathering pool. The dogs were having a great time running around and playing. Sal and I decided to sneak away from the dogs while they were distracted, playing with each other in the pool of water.

Up from the pool was a wooden bridge that went over the brook. We crossed the bridge and proceeded to call the dogs in an excitable tone of voice. They ran up from the pool, with Sam in the lead, to find their owners. Sam crossed the bridge first. Duke kicked in his speed, trying to keep up with Sam. He wasn't able to control the turn onto the bridge and went flying into the brook. Sal and I couldn't stop laughing. If only we had a picture of that event.

Memorable times with a dog can be a great reward in life—a reward I call "Captured Moments!"

Knight (a Doberman Love Story)

ONE AFTERNOON, MY veterinarian and good friend, Dr. Evan Dribbon, phoned me. Whenever I encountered any medical emergencies with my dogs, I could always count on my friend to be there for me, so when he asked if I would be interested in adopting an eight-month-old Doberman, although a little apprehensive, I went to take a look at the Doberman pincher.

Nitro was a handsome Dobie boy with a regal appearance. His life with his previous owner wasn't a happy one. His environment was a body shop with loud noises and other undesirable surroundings. I believe he was yelled at, and perhaps someone even hit him. What else would have caused him to bite? There were many tools around, which could have caused his broken leg by hitting him with anger, and I truly believe this is what happened.

When I arrived at Dr. Dribbon's office, Nitro was standing with a cast wrapped around his right hind leg. Dr. Dribbon had repaired the leg fracture the day before, but when the owner took the dog back to the shop, Nitro had bitten him. An employee of the shop was ordered to take Nitro back to the vet and have him euthanized. When I took the leash, Nitro growled, but I knew that he couldn't maneuver quick enough to bite me. What Dr. Dribbon hadn't mentioned was that Nitro had already bitten thirteen people.

The first of Nitro's many saves was the fact that the owner was not present with the dog to sign a waiver to have him euthanized. This gave Dr. Dribbon some leeway to try to place the dog with me, and so I was to give Nitro his second chance.

Little did I know, at the time, that the process of understanding this Dobie boy was soon to change my dog training career forever!

I changed Nitro's name to Knight. And while in my care, he slowly settled into a normal, loving Dobie life.

After only ten years in the training business, I hadn't fully taken the time to understand the Doberman breed. My niece, Michele, and I began to obedience train him. Michele had a unique connection with Dobermans and was able to communicate well enough to gain positive results.

Training was difficult at first since Knight wasn't very trusting of people. Walking him, feeding him, and speaking softly all helped in the rehabilitation program. This interaction allowed me to communicate more effectively when teaching Knight the obedience training. Aggressive dogs have to learn discipline, and the quicker this is programmed, the less chance of Michele and me being bitten. As a professional dog trainer, you have to demonstrate leadership (alpha status). This can only be firmly accomplished by using discipline with love.

I incorporated the correction "*no*" into the training method. Redirecting Knight, after the correction, was instrumental in order to gain his confidence in me. Redirect is a positive command followed after a *no* correction. If you correct and redirect, you will gain respect! This method was essential in order to gain control over Knight.

Each time I redirected Knight into a command, I used positive reinforcement with a lot of praise by using soft voice tones, especially when teaching Knight the heel command. Heel is similar to "come when called," which required the dog having enough trust and confidence to join up with me. His joining up is represented in heel, walking at my left side without pulling, and "come" is when called, followed by sitting in front of me.

After programming Knight during our one-on-one training sessions, our bond gradually became stronger. Ironically, at the time, I didn't have any desire to keep him as my personal dog. My feelings were that he would make an excellent protection dog for a qualified owner.

When Knight was around a year old, a reverend called me and asked if I had a qualified protection dog to sell. He went on to tell me that he is Black and moved into a White neighborhood, and consequently, someone tried to burn his house down. The reverend arrived at the kennel, met Knight, and prayed over him. When they left together, I thought Knight would have a loving home to live in for the rest of his life. Two weeks later, I received a call from the reverend, saying that Knight grabbed his daughter's arm when she attempted to sit next to him on the couch, and therefore he could not keep him. I told the reverend to bring Knight back, and I would replace him with another dog.

I decided to rent Knight out for guard duty. His first and last job was an empty house that needed protection over a two-day weekend. On the following Monday morning, I picked Knight up and put him into the passenger seat of my Volvo. While stopping at a red light, I looked over at Knight, and he, in return, leaned over and gave me a big lick on my face! I then placed my right arm over his shoulder and said, "You look pretty good sitting there next to me, so from now on, you are going to be my Dobie boy!" In that instant, without realizing the importance of this captured moment, I became "Doberized."

This bonding with Knight was one of my greatest dog-ownership experiences. I proved using love and determination that my method works on the hardest behavioral problem of all: aggressive behavior! Knight bonded with me, making him very protective. Many times he rode with me while serving clients in obedience training and checking up on security dog locations. On several occasions, he backed down intruders, saving me from harm. Whether it was the guy threatening to pull me out of my van or the guy at the schoolyard, coming toward me with a baseball bat, Knight was truly an intimidating Dobie, who prevented any threat to my life. I loved him! Knight was definitely the perfectly trained protection dog.

Later in his life, Knight became severely ill, with a bleeding prostrate. Dr. Dribbon met me at the hospital at 10:00 p.m. My dear friend operated on him until 2:00 a.m. and saved Knight once again. After the surgery, Knight became incontinent. I invented my own diaper system, consisting of white grooming towels and Velcro strips. These enabled me to perform quick changes when necessary. Knight passed away four years later due to a heart attack brought on from cardiomyopathy, a prevalent heart disease in Doberman pinschers. Knight was truly a gift for twelve years. I miss him dearly!

Ode to Knight
Written on January 16, 1987

Early morning on the rise
A sleepy boy with staring eyes
Shaking, stamping, a sneeze makes three
You try earnestly to awaken me
Your breath vibrating in my ear
My hand responds to a touch of hair
A cold nose pushed into my face
You patiently await another move to take place
Connecting eyes, a hug or two
I start my day, knowing I am loved by you!

Training notes:

It's significant to remember that aggressive behavior is the most difficult behavioral problem in dogs. Supremacy is only gained through a proven method in obedience communication.

Understanding why a dog is aggressive is paramount. Factors such as inherited traits, early puppyhood, adolescent environment, harsh treatment training from a bogus trainer, breed type, length of time of previous negative conditioning, possessiveness (mainly the prey-driven scent in raw meat and bones), and territorial motion-driven behavior can all play a part in aggressive behaviors. Fortunately, in Knight's case, my knowledge background helped tremendously in understanding why his behavior was unstable. Knight needed someone who could give him a secure environment and a training method relevant to control his behavior. That someone fortunately was me.

Trust in correcting the aggression, maintaining alpha status, positive reinforcement, playing, walks, feeding, brushing, and plenty of love all worked toward Knight's rehabilitation. *I personally never had any doubt and always made sure that my commitment was intact.*

Knight was one of my more profound endeavors in a long history of behavioral training accomplishments. My confidence was made stronger, knowing that I could help many dog owners rehabilitate aggressive behaviors.

Autumn (My Red Dobie Boy)

SOMETIME IN THE year of 2007, I had left some cash on the dining room table for my wife. Later in the day, I asked my wife if she saw or had taken the money. She said, "I thought I saw it earlier," but it was not on the table. After looking for the money and coming up empty, she still needed the cash. I gave her more money, suspecting that she might have misplaced the original cash that I had left for her. Needless to say, I was not happy about the whole thing. The following morning, I began my daily routine of picking up dog poop in the backyard. At the time, I owned two Dobermans, and each had a designated area where they defecated. While approaching Autumn's droppings, I noticed President Jackson staring up at me, deeply embedded in dog poop! I frantically parted the poop with a couple of sticks, and there it all was, three twenty-dollar bills and one fifty. I carefully washed the money and then put it all in the microwave for a few seconds to dry. The majority of the bills had to be taped, although not much could be done with the fifty-dollar bill.

I decided to bring the money with me to the bank, hoping that the bills could be replaced. Later in the day, I broke the news to my wife, along with an apology. After all, I did suspect that she misplaced the money. This type of accusation is not uncommon among men, husbands in general. We have a tendency to ask our better half where they put whatever we can't find. In this case, it was my fault as I left the money where Autumn could get it.

"Honey," I said, "what do I tell the bank personal?" After all, they know that I'm a dog trainer. I can't tell them the truth! This would make me look bad! My wife suggested I tell them that the money somehow got into the garbage compactor.

The next day, I arrived at the bank and proceeded with explaining my money dilemma to an understanding bank representative. I showed her the money and proceeded to tell her a fib. A roaming manager was summoned over to our desk, and I explained the situation.

Before starting my transactions, the bank representative asked me, "How are those garbage compactors, Kurt?" Now, if you ever watched Judge Judy on TV, she always said, "If you lie, you better have a good memory!" I lied and, of course, have little or no knowledge on how good a garbage compactor really is. Besides, I don't even own one. I asked for a pencil and paper, and on it I wrote, "I lied to you. I found the money in dog poop." As the bank management personnel approached with my replaced money, I asked my investment representative to please not mention what truly occurred. The three twenties were replaced, but the fifty was unreplaceable. Grant was too "pooped" out to be replaced! When I arrived home, I immediately went out back to go through any remaining poop, hoping to find more parts to the fifty-dollar bill. After a few seconds of intense labor, a little voice in my head said the following: "Kurt, didn't you just make a substantial amount of money on your house sale, and so why in the world do you need to look in dog poop for the rest of the fifty-dollar bill?" If General Grant were alive today, he would be very unhappy if part of him went south!

Autumn's redemption 2010

Soon after this event, on a quiet April morning, as usual, I was outside, doing what is an everyday routine: picking up dog poop. At the far end of the yard, Autumn and my female Dobie, Shade, were running around a wooden pallet that was covered with a tarp, protecting lawn equipment. I thought there was probably a raccoon or an opossum under the tarp and quickly commanded them away from the area of interest. My first instinct was to leave well enough alone. A day passed, and once again, there was a commotion in the same area. But this time, it was just Autumn. He was crying and sniffing the tarp with relentless determination. As I approached the tarp, I heard a faint "meow, meow!" I quickly removed the tarp and the lawn equipment and lifted up the pallet. There lay an orange and white kitten in a bed of leaves. I gently lifted him up, walked a few feet, and decided to put him back on the bed of leaves. I estimated the kitten to be around ten days old and contemplated placing him back under the pallet, where his mother could find him. As I placed the kitten down, I noticed two white feathers a few feet away from him. In the Christian faith, a white dove is represented as the Holy Spirit. I assumed that the two white feathers found near the kitten's birthplace was that of a dove.

Knowing, at that moment, this was a miracle, I brought the kitten into the house and placed him into a box with a warm blanket. I then placed the box into a small dog cage to prevent my dogs from disturbing him while sleeping. The next important step was to contact my pet supply store for formula and a feeding bottle. They informed me that they had the formula but not the bottle. This little guy needed nourishment. I would use an eyedropper to feed him until there was time to locate a feeding bottle. My wife arrived home from work and immediately took charge of feeding the kitten. She reminded me of another pet store nearby, and I was able to purchase a feeding bottle, along with more kitten formula. During feeding time, we would place the kitten on his back and lay him between our knees. After feedings, Autumn would lick him to stimulate defecation.

Autumn became the kitten's surrogate mother. This wonderful, loving Dobie male became persistent in keeping his son clean from head to tail. Autumn also kept our female Dobie, Shade, from the kitten. He only had to growl one time, and Shade quickly backed away from him. My wife, Ruth, named the kitten Dove after telling her about the white feathers near the pallet. There were many more captured moments between Autumn and Dove. They played, slept, and later ate meals together. This heartwarming event still entertains our household today. Autumn, I forgive you on behalf of your loyal, loving devotion toward Dove! It was all worth the fifty dollars!

Training notes:

The behavior that Autumn exhibited is called surfing. Large breeds, like Dobermans, have more of an advantage when engaging in this behavior. They are able to reach countertops, tables, or any other surface that is tailored for their height. The top of the list for desired surfing is food that is left out on counters and tabletops. Also, items that have your scent on them will attract a dog enough to encourage surfing—in my case, money. If a table or any higher structures are near a window or door, the dog may surf if he/she becomes excited by a distraction, such as a knock on the door or people or animals walking onto the property. Out of aggressive frustration, dogs will redirect on anything that is close and available to them, such as clothing, shoes, or houseplants.

The solution to this behavioral problem is to keep all tables, counters clear of anything that will attract your dog to surf. Like most behavioral problems, you may always apply the *no* correction or use the off-leash throw chain correction if you catch your dog in the act of surfing. Snappy trainers are also a good deterrent for this behavior. Remember, if there is nothing for your dog to take, he will eventually become desensitized from this behavior. On the other hand, if left to surf, it will become a reinforced behavior and be much more difficult to break and control. Remember, dogs are creatures of habit, and the longer surfing lasts, the more it becomes reinforced. Recognizing that this inherited trait—surfing—is genetically programmed, remember, your best friend is just being a dog!

Leroy (Saving a Lost Dog)

THIS EPISODE STARTED on a cold, damp, rainy April morning while I was driving toward a dog training lesson. As I was turning off the service road to enter the parkway, a small brown dog suddenly appeared. He was just sitting there under a tree, shivering, wet, and sad looking. I rolled down the window, and he just gazed at me with sympathetic brown eyes. I spoke to him softly, saying, "What are you doing here in the rain? Are you a lost doggie?" I couldn't leave him in the rain, so I got out of my van and walked over to this shivering little dog, picked him up, and off we went to my dog training lesson.

My client had a few young ladies working for him, and I felt, perhaps one of them would want to take this dog home. The young ladies had little or no interest in adopting him; therefore, I brought the little guy home with me.

I spent the following weeks dedicated to bringing this dog back to health. He received his inoculations, was wormed, and put on a healthy diet. The truth was that I really didn't want this dog! My pack consisted of four German shepherds, which at the time, I felt represented me well in the dog world.

I reviewed lost and found sections in leading newspapers, notified local pounds, veterinary hospitals, and kennels in earnest looking for the dog's owner. All my efforts led nowhere, and so this little brown dog became part of my shepherd pack.

Day by day, it became more evident to me that my dogs were accepting him into the family. It was fun to watch them play and interact with each other. Around this time, I heard a new song on the radio, "Leroy Brown." Leroy became his name.

Leroy recovered and was a healthy, happy, and spoiled little dog. I trained him with just enough leash and collar work to program basic obedience. All I needed was for him to be happy and obey basic commands. He accepted off-leash training more readily, and when I called the shepherds, Leroy followed along with them.

The only behavioral problem I had with Leroy was his eliminating in the house. It was always in the same area, the center of my front room. Six months prior to finding Leroy, I had taken up the carpets in the room and replaced them with linoleum flooring. This time, I was ready to catch him in the act of defecating. I had a general idea what time of the day Leroy would circle around in the front room to relieve himself. I hid in the bathroom located twenty feet down the hallway. The timing was perfect. I corrected him as soon as he stopped circling. I tossed the shake can simultaneously with the "no" correction. It landed right under Leroy, and he never defecated in the house again!

Leroy was loved not only by me but by many people and dogs who came in contact with him, especially an Afghan hound named Benji. Leroy lived a long and happy fifteen years! We truly found each other, and I often wondered who adopted who!

Training notes:

Whether you find, adopt, rescue, or purchase a dog, you should always try to find out as much as you can about the dog's background. This will help immensely in communicating with your new friend. Knowing the dog's previous environmental conditioning is important in solving any existing behavioral problems.

Be patient, and give ample time for your new friend to adapt to his or her new home. Environmental adjustments take around three weeks. After this time period, a dog usually is adjusted to her new environment. This three-week adjustment period focuses on acclimating to his new home, existing pets, and members of the family.

The main focus should be on coexisting with other household pets, especially older dogs, in order to prevent aggressive behavior. It is important that communication is consistent with all family members when interacting with their new adopted dog.

Seek professional help from a behaviorist dog trainer for obedience communication training. Make sure he or she is qualified to solve any existing behavioral problems, communication issues, and elimination prevention, if necessary.

Harley (Home at Last)

THE POPULATION OF unsung heroes includes a countless number of selfless people, who dedicate their time and effort to help save dogs. I've had the honor of being associated with many of these people during my dog training career. One person who specifically comes to mind is Cindy, a dog trainer who worked for me when this special rescue took place.

At the time, Cindy was also working part-time for a veterinarian on Long Island. During one of her workdays, a woman walked into the office with three animals she wanted euthanized. This heartless woman was going through a divorce and didn't want to have anything to do with the family animals. The smaller of the two dogs was euthanized because of old age, but the other two pets, Harley, a Labrador mix, and Shadow, a cat, had a more fortunate outcome.

Cindy called me, and I took Harley and Shadow. Whenever any rescue arrived, I would carefully evaluate them. Harley had an existing condition called possessive-aggressive behavior. This behavior was discovered when I threw a tennis ball and, after he retrieved it, refused giving it up. When I went to take the ball from him, he would growl. At the time, there was another rescue dog in the kennel; his name was DJ, a small chow mix. Harley and DJ played without incident until DJ tried to grab Harley's tennis ball. Harley attempted to bite DJ, and although it wasn't an attack intending to inflict real damage, it was, however, enough aggression to promote serious concern.

Discipline with love would be necessary in order to fully ready Harley for adoption. After three weeks of intensive training, Harley was ready to be evaluated for adoption. I was able to control Harley using DJ and the tennis ball in distraction work. I felt secure that Harley's possessive aggression could be dealt with by applying my method of training. This method would have to be passed on to anyone interested in adopting Harley. My final test was for me to be able to remove a ball from Harley's mouth, condition him to leave it, followed by retrieving on command. After successfully completing this test, I took Harley to be groomed, as it was evident that he was ready to be adopted.

The shop owner, Susan, also runs her own rescue organization. She suggested I leave Harley in her care for a day in hopes of placing him for adoption. I felt that Susan was qualified in selecting the right people to adopt Harley. During his stay there, a young couple showed interest in him. They said that they would call later in the day with their decision.

As the day progressed, a middle-aged woman showed interest in Harley. The young couple who showed earlier interest, never called back, but Susan felt the woman would be a more suitable prospect for the adoption. I was excited when receiving the phone call from Susan, telling me that Harley had been adopted!

The woman who adopted Harley left him in her house and went shopping. She came home to find that Harley tried to eat his way through the back door of the house. I blamed myself for not being there to personally evaluate and train the potential new owner.

I picked up Harley from the woman's house and brought him home. I decided to keep working with Harley every day in obedience, which is essential for maintaining positive control.

Finally, the day arrived when a family of four came to see Harley. The family included a husband, wife, eight-year-old son, and eleven-year-old daughter. This seemed like the perfect match for a successful adoption. Harley gravitated immediately toward the young eleven-year-old daughter. The family all seemed to like Harley, especially after playing ball with him. Yes, he would give up the ball without showing any dominance!

All the hard work I put into training Harley to retrieve and release the tennis ball paid off. The entire family joined in learning the basic commands sit, stay, heel, come, down, and the "No" correction. Harley was willing to please all the family members who handled him on leash. It was as though he knew this was the family that he would spend the rest of his life with. This was Harley's lucky day. This wholesome family wanted to adopt him.

I worked with all the family members in obedience and included using the no correction in order to be sure they maintained alpha control. We also practiced the release command: "Drop it" with Harley to control him from falling back into possessive aggression behavior. I made it perfectly clear what could happen if any outsider approached Harley abruptly, especially when he had a ball or any object in his mouth. They were also instructed to never allow anyone outside of the family to try and take any object from him.

I then set up an appointment schedule to expand the obedience lessons while Harley was adjusting to his new environment. After an appropriate amount of time passed, I began to feel more secure that Harley and his new family were on the road toward a successful relationship.

The eleven-year-old daughter and Harley developed a very close relationship. Harley slept in her bed and always wanted to be close to her. His new friend could take anything from him without showing aggression.

Some weeks later, I received a phone call from the mother, saying she was sorry, but she needed me to take Harley back. My response was one of disbelief!

After all the training and preparation to place Harley into this wonderful family, it was all over due to one mistake. Harley had retrieved a glove that was dropped by the daughter's girlfriend. Her mother gave the order for Harley to release the glove, and she then gave it back to the girlfriend. This same girl decided to try to repeat what she saw. She threw her glove onto the ground for Harley to pick up. When she approached Harley to take the glove from his mouth, Harley bit her! This was just what I tried desperately to avoid from happening!

The mother did confess that it was her fault and that she should have been watching Harley interact with a nonfamily member. The daughter was heartbroken and wasn't anywhere in sight the day I arrived to pick up Harley.

After some time, a middle-aged couple came to see Harley. The man never stopped speaking about his last dog named Red Wolf, but they definitely wanted Harley. I decided to gamble once again and placed him with this couple. My intuition went one way, while my heart pulled in the opposite direction, but I was hopeful that this man and woman would be the right choice for Harley. After a couple of weeks, I received numerous phone calls from the husband, complaining that Harley was not like his previous dog. He went on to say that Red Wolf would come when he was called and always obeyed him. I explained that Harley needed more time to adjust to his new surroundings; however, he insisted on giving Harley back to me.

Arrangements were made to bring Harley back to my kennel once again! This thoughtless man was met by my wife as he pulled up in front of my home. My wife, Ruth, asked for the leash, took Harley, and told the man to leave.

After multiple homes without any grounded stability, I was concerned for Harley's psychological well-being, and I began to realize that his home was with us. During this period of time, my sister and brother-in-law were renting my house on the kennel property. They had two dogs that were in their senior years. One soon passed away, and the other, Betsy, didn't have long before she, too, would pass. My sister, Gertrude, had already developed a relationship with Harley while helping me out with the kennel chores. She decided to bring Harley from the kennel and place him into the attached room of the garage. This led to a significant bond between Gertrude and Harley. In a short period of time, Harley's dream came true; he was taken into the house with my sister, brother-in-law, and nephew.

We were happy to have Harley in the family! Soon thereafter, Harley turned out to be a hero! My nephew, Chris, has juvenile diabetes. One night, Chris went into hypoglycemic shock (reaction to low blood sugar), and if not addressed quickly, he could have gone into a diabetic coma. Harley realized Chris was in a crisis and went into my sister's bedroom and awakened her. If it wasn't for Harley, Chris may have been in serious trouble. Of course, Gertrude was

Harley's true love, and they bonded for the next five years until Harley passed away. Harley never showed aggression and lived to be a loyal, loving dog.

Training notes:

Careful evaluation of all adopted dogs should only be made by an experienced professional dog trainer. It is important that adopted dogs be matched with the correct humans. Few dogs would never have ended up without psychological problems after being dragged through so many environments. Multi-environments can cause separation anxiety!

Professional behavioral communication training is necessary in order to fully understand your dog's personality! This training process allows you to fully ascertain and correct any psychological-behavioral problem the dog may have. In Harley's case, it required me to take my time evaluating him before training. I knew that in his former environment, there were other pets and children. Harley's possessive-aggressive behavior definitely developed due to all the competition that surrounded him. Therefore, it was my goal to concentrate on discipline without allowing aggression.

With over thirty years of professional dog training experience, keeping an aggressive dog under my care would be the only solution in correcting the behavior. My method requires that the trainer has alpha status. Once a dog understands you are in charge, then you begin to desensitize him from all behavioral problems—in Harley's case, aggressive-possessive behavior.

Harley is living proof that perseverance, along with a proven method of training, is the only way to control negative behaviors, remembering always to use discipline with love!

Lance and Max (Rescue Dogs with a Purpose)

THIS MEMORABLE STORY is about two German shepherds, Lance and Max. They were both relinquished into my adoption/protection program sometime in 1988. As with other dogs I have saved, Lance and Max received a careful evaluation, followed by a comprehensive training program in obedience communication. A trained dog has a better chance of ending up in a secure environment.

After six months of pretraining for both protection and guard/security, I knew Max and Lance would make a provocative security team for their new owners, an attorney and his wife. They wanted a security team to guard their property and for personal protection. The attorney and his wife lived on an estate with a house and adjoining law office. The courtyard had a connecting entrance to two acres of grounds for Max and Lance to protect.

I had to make certain that Lance and Max would prohibit any intruders from entering the estate and would also be trained to protect all family and work personnel. The new owners were taught the obedience and protection commands.

I waited a few days for Max and Lance to become adjusted to their new home before beginning any security or protection training.

Max and Lance had already been pretrained at my kennel. It was imperative that I reinforce the training in their new environment.

On the selected day to see how Max and Lance would respond to an intruder, I chose one of the young men that volunteered at my kennel to assist in the training. He was fully trained in agitation and, for his safety, wore personal protection equipment, which included a full training suit.

The training started out by having the agitator simulate an intruder while hiding at one end of the estate. I then leashed both dogs and encouraged them to find the intruder. When we arrived at the general area where the intruder was, the dogs alerted, found the intruder, and each dog grabbed an arm.

Happy with the result, I decided to unleash the dogs for the next attack. I had to know Max and Lance would do the job while off leash without any assistance from me. Both dogs attacked the agitator and knocked him to the ground with a secure grip on his arm and leg! Needless to say, he was clearly upset with me for allowing the dogs to attack him without a leash on! I informed him that they won't be working on a leash, and it was important for me to see the dogs do the off-leash attack!

Max and Lance were happy at their new home. They were given home-cooked meals, soft beds, and much love and attention.

After approximately five years, I received a call, informing me that the estate was sold and that they were moving. My client asked me to pick up the dogs and board them until they could settle into their new home.

I hadn't seen the dogs in five years, but knowing that my training of Max and Lance in obedience communication would afford me their respect, I decided to pick up the dogs by myself. Also, I knew that once they picked up my scent, there would be less concern of being attacked. Max and I bonded in the training program, and he always respected me as the alpha. Max was alpha over Lance, and I knew, if Max accepted me, Lance would follow.

On the day of my arrival, I parked my van in the courtyard. The grounds surrounded a huge home with a long-constructed unit connected at right angle to the house. This unit was the law office with the connecting entrance to the grounds.

The family and office employees were all watching and totally concerned that the dogs would attack me! I tried my best to ensure all concerned not to worry. Knowledge, confidence, and years of experience were all part of my dog-training profession.

Both dogs were located at the far end of the property. They were unaware of me entering the yard until I yelled out, "Max, Lance!" I waited until the dogs were within fifty feet of me and then proceeded to drop low toward the ground. Next, I began saying their names, using a soft whimpering tone. Max suddenly went from fierce protection dog to "I'm happy to see you" mode! I knew, at that instant, he had picked up on my scent. His charge knocked me over, followed by wet licks all over my face. Wow, what a tremendous greeting! Lance ran down the cellar steps, avoiding anything to do with me. He always overrespected me as alpha. The parting of the dogs made the attorney's wife more upset than anyone else on the premises. After all, she made sure Max and Lance had cooked meals and soft bedding!

After a few weeks had passed, I received a call from the attorney, saying that the town ordinances would not allow any fencing erected on their new property. Consequently, I was to keep the dogs until they decided what the next step would be. That next step became a permanent stay for Max and Lance to board with me.

During the early period of boarding, the attorney's wife would bring blankets, toys, and food. Her bonding with the dogs was evident, and I had to tell her that it would be better for the dogs psychologically if she stopped the visits. The dogs had to readjust to their new environment. I promised that Max and Lance would be well taken care of—lots of play, good food, and love! Max passed away two years later, followed by Lance a year after.

Training notes:

All rescue dogs were totally trained. I had to be able to handle any dog used for protection purposes. If I sold a dog, it had to be fully obedience trained. A trained dog had a much easier chance of relocating into a secure, loving home. Training definitely paid off for me in the case of Lance and Max. Although you could say, my scent went a long way!

Trevor (My Sister's Rescue Dog)

TREVOR, HALF CHIHUAHUA and half whippet, was a rescued dog from Last Hope Animal Rescue organization. This dedicated rescue organization is located on Long Island, New York, and does outstanding work getting homes for abandoned dogs. Trevor is one of the lucky dogs who was adopted by my sister, Gertrude. Of course, I was selected to train this cute little dog. I told my sister to give Trevor a few weeks to adjust to his new environment. During this adjustment period, drama struck. One of Trevor's new owners (Chris, my nephew) and I had returned to Trevor's new home after lunch one day. I opened the front door. And while making sure it stayed open for my nephew, I simultaneously opened the side door, which entered into the living room of the house. Two doors open to the outside gave Trevor an escape route. This was not a responsive dog. Trevor was oblivious to stopping, coming, or sitting and staying. He put his nose to the ground and ran like the wind into the adjoining neighborhood.

Praying, I jumped into my Durango, and the chase was on! Trevor, being half whippet, ran extremely fast. After a few blocks, I was able to pull up ahead of the direction he was going. I got out of my vehicle and proceeded to squat down and call him in a light tone of voice. This got his attention, and he ran over to me. I went to grab the collar under his neck and missed.

Having missed him the first time, I knew that Trevor would avoid coming to me, knowing that I would attempt to grab his collar!

There were a few people in the chase, but Trevor wouldn't have any interest in coming to them. After a ten-minute chase, I lost sight of him, until my nephew called me on the cell phone to inform me that Trevor had headed back toward the house. I proceeded toward home, but Trevor passed the house and was heading toward a main road. I managed to beat Trevor to the road and proceeded to halt all cars. I blasted my horn while standing out in the middle of Deer Park Ave. I stopped all traffic while Trevor scooted across to the other side. Once he started running away from the main road, I stayed with him in a parallel position. When Trevor stopped running, I stopped and opened my car door, called him, and into the Durango, he jumped.

What a relief! At that moment, I promised that Trevor would come when called! Oh, I forgot to mention that my prayers were answered! The following day after this incident, Trevor was enrolled into my obedience training program. I promised my sister that this near tragedy would never happen again!

Training notes:

Rescue dogs inevitably will come to you with a previous history of life experiences. Some of these experiences may have been good, but the majority are usually bad!

People working in shelters will pass as much information about a rescue dog's history before you adopt. If possible, a rescue organization will spend time learning the previous history of a dog. Of course, in many cases, the truth may never be known! As in Trevor's case, he probably ran away from a previous owner. This behavior is easily corrected when a dog is properly trained to come when called. The majority of negative behaviors can be turned around using discipline with love!

Modifying previous learned behaviors may be very difficult due to puppy mill breeding, lack of socialization, emotional damage, genetic code, and early environmental associations Find a professional dog trainer who is qualified in understanding behavioral problems. Experience in knowing why a dog behaves a certain way and in return using a method of communication similar to dog language, you found the professional dog trainer you need!

Blackie (Innate Guarding of Food with the Scent of Prey)

THE FOLLOWING INCIDENT occurred in the summer of 2003. Anyone who has an aggressive dog should pay special attention to what is about to unfold later in this story. As like many of my short stories, this is related to dog training in a client's home.

Tom and Patty asked me to evaluate their two Labrador retrievers Buddy and Blackie for obedience communication. The dogs showed no sign of dominance or aggression toward people or other dogs. The six-week training started and ended with favorable results.

A short time later, I received a phone call from Tom, saying that Blackie bit Patty and their granddaughter, Nicky. Deeply concerned, I desperately tried to calm Tom down and told him that I would do my best to deal with this incident. After allowing Tom to vent his frustration, I finally convinced him to wait until I could evaluate Blackie before he took any action.

I first had to gain perspective as to what exactly led up to the incident in the first place. Some readers may be old enough to remember a famous TV detective, Columbo. Like this TV character, I had to figure out what caused Blackie to commit this heinous crime. Aggressive behavior can be complex, and I needed a detailed explanation of what led up to the attack in order to gain a clear understanding of what triggered the biting.

It was supposed to be a wonderful morning with Patty and her eight-year-old granddaughter, Nicky. They were both in the kitchen area, cooking breakfast and enjoying their grandma-granddaughter time together. Nicky decided to pick up Blackie's empty food dish, which was ten to twelve feet from the stove. Blackie was still near the dish as Nicky reached over him, attempting to remove it from the floor. (Note that one of the more frequent actions of human error, "standing over" was committed.)

I informed Pat that Nicky reached over the top of Blackie, and this was probably why her granddaughter was bitten. Patty replied, "Nicky has removed Blackie's and Buddy's dish from the floor on several occasions without ever seeing any indication of aggressive behavior."

Since an empty food dish shouldn't have triggered a bite, I asked Patty if she was still feeding the same dog food prior to this incident. Patty replied that she had just started feeding the dogs a rolled-up frozen raw beef dog food that her veterinarian recommended and sold. The vet told her it was the same meat that is fed to zoo animals. He also told her that this food was more nutritious for her dogs and very similar to the food that they would consume in their wild state. Ouch! No wonder little Nicky was attacked! Not only did she stand over Blackie, but there still were remains of scented meat in the dish.

Patty told me that after she realized what was taking place, she charged toward Blackie and hit him over his head with a frying pan. Blackie quickly retreated downstairs to avoid any further anger from Patty. Nicky was taken upstairs where Patty attended to her wound and then ordered Nicky to stay in the bedroom. Patty then felt guilty for hitting Blackie over the head and decided to try and make up with him.

While sitting on the bottom half of the stairs, she called Blackie. When Blackie came within range, Patty proceeded to reach over his head to give make-up hugs and kisses. Blackie bit her on the lip! Patty made a costly mistake by reaching over Blackie's head. In her mind, she wanted to make up with Blackie after hitting him with a frying pan, but Blackie still was not fully trusting Patty and perceived her attempt at affection as a threat. Pat's frying pan aggression still lingered in Blackie's mind, therefore reaching over his head increased the threat, resulting in a bite!

I fully realized why this all happened and understood why Tom was extremely angry! After everyone was calm and ready to hear my professional view, I instructed, "*No more raw meat!*" I continued on giving Tom and Patty an education in dog psychology, which included a concrete explanation on the reason for Blackie's aggression!

I went on to explain that in a dog's *wild state*, they coexist as a pack through an innate method of communication called the pecking order. In the pecking order, lower ranking dogs become submissive to the hierarchy of members of the pack. High ranking members will demonstrate this by nipping and growling in order to keep lower-ranking member subordinates controlled within the pack. Old and young members are most likely to be controlled within the pack. Nicky, being a child, is considered a lower-ranking young member in the pecking order.

I reiterated how important it is to program the "no" correction that they learned in the training program but admittedly had not reinforced it at all in the posttraining. I knew that if Patty had been more conscientious in following through with the dog training program by reinforcing the "no" correction, this incident could have been prevented. Nicky, being a child, has the lowest ranking in the family pack; therefore, it was up to the adults of the family to control Blackie. Also, Patty should have removed the dish, provided she had maintained alpha status.

We reviewed the method to make sure Blackie respected her authority and associated her as being in charge. I worked with Pat and Blackie to be sure he respected her status and that she had regained control, combining discipline with love.

In the end, all turned out well without any more attacks.

Training notes:

Raw meat is similar to the prey a dog would consume in his *wild state*. And dogs, through genetic programming, will protect this resource. The combination of standing over and grabbing the dish was a grave mistake.

In all cases of aggressive behavior, your dog has to respect you in order to prevent aggression from guarding his food. This will assure you that this innate behavior never inadvertently surfaces in the future. Additionally, male dogs will generally show alpha status over females quicker than they will over males.

It cannot be emphasized more strongly that the family dog(s) be trained through a comprehensive training program and the owners establish that they are in charge (alpha) by consistently applying the "no" correction. This is the only answer to all behavioral problems, particularly with aggressive behavior.

Your personal dog should never bite you! Applying discipline with love, a method where your dog trusts and looks up to you as the pack leader, will transcend his innate tendencies and develop into a well-behaved dog. Discipline means that when you give the "no" correction, your best friend will stop immediately from whatever negative behavior you intend to stop him from doing. This method should prevent an aggressive incident, even if you are standing over your dog.

When you establish a coexistent relationship, he or she will never hesitate to join up with you when receiving your command. Never forget to reward your dog with love. Hugs, kisses, and treats for good behavior all contribute to developing trust and security.

Foods that can contribute to aggressive behavior are raw meat, bones, rawhide, and any other foods with the scent of the prey.

In dog communication, standing over indicates one dog showing dominance over another. A higher-ranking dog will demonstrate standing over by placing his/her paw over the body, head, or neck, or mounting another dog. Lower-ranking dogs will submit to standing over, avoiding confrontation. Likewise, human errors in standing over are approaching over the top of a dog's head, grabbing his collar or removing a resource from his mouth. A high percentage of children, as well as some adults, make the grave mistake of reaching over a dog's head to hug or kiss him!

Standing over aggression is more prevalent with strange dogs or a family dog not respecting a family member. The method of prevention is to train your dog using discipline with love. If you correct and redirect your dog into a positive behavior, you will gain his respect! Never yell or hit! Be persistent. Appropriately program the "no" within the structure of the training program, and apply it when needed. Continue the journey. Love your dog!

Alfie (the Poodle Who
Refused to Heel)

THERE WERE NUMEROUS occasions during my career that required concentration as to why a particular behavior was imminent. The following is a story of one of my many unique dog training experiences.

Alfie was a white standard poodle, approximately two years old. He seemed to be a very shy dog and showed extreme avoidance of the leash.

I had been recommended to the family by a renowned Long Island, New York artist. I had trained three of her dogs, and the recommendation was made based on positive results. There was no question in my mind; I had to come through on a difficult, if not impossible, behavioral problem.

When I first met Alfie, he seemed very shy and totally avoided me. I soon learned that Alfie had a traumatic experience with a previous dog trainer. This particular trainer had difficulty teaching Alfie the heel command (walking on the left side) when working outside on the street. Alfie's owner informed me that on several occasions, the previous trainer became totally frustrated and dragged Alfie while attempting to teach the heel command. It was apparent that she had no clue as to how to motivate Alfie to perform the heel command. Instead, she used force!

I instructed an adult member of the family to put a collar on Alfie, hook the leash to the collar, and hand the leash to me. Because of his prior training experience, Alfie refused to have any part of me holding the leash. To make him more comfortable, I instructed the mother of the family in leash obedience communication. It was essential that I instructed her on how to use discipline with love when teaching the commands. We started with the sit-stay command when the front door was opened to the outside. This way, the correction *no* would easily be programmed into Alfie's head when attempting to bolt out the front door! The trial here is in hope that Alfie focuses on any movement presented outside. This is referred to as tunnel vision! The desire is that this innate distraction will help absorb any correction used to prevent Alfie from bolting out the door. This collar correction should help when teaching the heel command.

Alfie wanted no part of cooperating in the street. This was due to the traumatic experience he had from the previous training he received. I decided to pick Alfie up and carry him over to the adjacent block. This is a method I used many times, called area redirect.

Dogs act according to the environment they are in at the present time, and the street in the front of the house had been a bad experience for Alfie. Area redirect worked for me on numerous occasions, all except this one. This poodle wouldn't listen to the adults of the family when leashed outside. I tried in vain to instruct without me touching the leash, yet Alfie didn't seem to trust any adults.

When the family and I were in the backyard with Alfie, I noticed that Alfie did not hesitate on the recall command when the thirteen-year-old son called him. Mark had just recently received his bar mitzvah, and knowing this was the age of religious duty and responsibility, I decided to turn the training over to him. I said, "Mark, you are now a young man and are needed to help train Alfie. He trusts you more than the adults of the family. Therefore, would you be willing to learn how to teach Alfie to heel?" Mark agreed to my intuition and serendipity! My reward soon followed!

Knowing that "heel" and "come" were very similar led me to believe there was hope after all. I gave Mark the leash and guided him in teaching the heel command. Alfie felt completely secure in his backyard with a young adult training him. In a short period of time, Mark, with Alfie at his left side, performed the heel command in the street. There are times in my career when I truly feel blessed, and this was undoubtedly one of those times. Area redirect and the security of a young family member paid off!

Unfortunately, the previous dog trainer used crude methods without any positive results. I also replaced this trainer on another occasion to train a small dog. The owner showed me a video of her brushing the dog with a slicker brush. This type of brush is constructed of short metal bristles used to pull out the dog's loose undercoat. The dog was on a lead and growled every time the trainer began to brush him. The trainer received a bite when she picked the dog up to brush the other side. With that, she yanked this helpless dog back and forth into submission. This unprofessional dog trainer told her client that the dog shouldn't be growling when brushed and advised they should consider getting rid of the dog.

I also saw a video of a renowned dog trainer exhibiting the same brushing method on a small dog. In this case, he just accepted being bitten. Not accepting responsibility for the dog's actions, he also told the owner that the dog has aggressive behavior tendencies. A slicker brush was used on both of these dogs.

Training notes:

As with Alfie, not wanting to cooperate in the heel position, all dogs need to feel secure with you and your method of interacting. Dog owners or professionals should understand how dogs function and respect their feelings when giving commands, corrections, brushing, bathing, examining teeth, cleaning ears, bathing, car riding, or in any other condition where your dog may initially feel insecure. Never be abrupt when introducing any grooming tool to a dog. A slicker brush is safe when used correctly; however, caution is recommended when using this type of brush for the first time.

Always approach your dog slowly when introducing anything new. The back of the brush should be presented first. This way, the dog can sniff it without being pricked by the bristles. If your dog accepts the back of the brush, then gently touch a part of his back using a brushing motion. Once he/she accepts the touch of the back of the brush, slowly turn the brush over and lightly use the bristle side. Stop if your dog is not accepting the brushing and turn to the back side. Once again, allow your dog to sniff the nonbristle side and follow up with a treat. After a couple of follow-ups using this method, your dog should start accepting the brush.

Remember, using discipline with love is your key to success!

Bruno and Luke (and the Priests)

FATHER DAVIES, A priest at St. Joachim and Ann in Queens, New York, called to say that he and his associate, Father Lanning own two German shepherd mix dogs and would like to have them trained to be more controlled when we take them out for a walk. I introduced myself and additionally asked the routine dog behavior questions: age, gender, how long the dogs had been in their present environment, where they were purchased or rescued from, aggression profile, if both dogs get along with each other, and the main purpose for having two of these shepherd-type dogs?

Father Davies went on to tell me that the main reason for having the dogs was to protect the church from being robbed. The church had been robbed several times prior to having the dogs. Since having the dogs, the church had not been broken into, but there was a problem when he and Father Lanning took the dogs outside for a walk.

The two priests were out walking Bruno and Luke, when all of a sudden, Bruno leaped onto a man walking by and knocked him into a hedge. It happened so quickly that they didn't have time to react! Father Lanning ran over to try to assist the man who refused any help. In the days that followed, they received a phone call from the man claiming that his injury was serious and that due to his injury, he no longer could make love to his wife. Father Lanning and Davies were totally serious about what took place, and I had to quickly remind myself that this incident was no laughing matter. The heel lesson was going to play a significant role in preventing this from ever happening again. Furthermore, it was my understanding that the priest had to receive permission from their peers in the Catholic Church in order to have the dogs. Knowing the significance of this motivated me to complete a comprehensive training program, keeping Bruno and Luke with Father Davis and Father Lanning.

The lessons were successful, and all seemed to be working toward a positive outcome until Bruno began urinating while guarding the inside of the church! I quickly set up the elimination behavior program.

As part of the elimination method, I recommended to reward Bruno each time he made outside. The priests were given a special liver-based treat and instructed to present this to him right after elimination. This association, when giving a treat for eliminating outside, should encourage Bruno to relieve himself outdoors instead of in the church. During one of the training lessons, Father Davies replied that the method was working but that he needed a lot more treats. When I asked why he needed an abundance of treats, he replied, "Every time Bruno comes across a tree, johnnie pump, etc., he stops to determine whether or not he has any urine left in him!" Upon visiting Bruno, I was eyewitness to the urination event! Sure enough, every time Bruno stopped while Father Davies was walking him, he picked up his leg, sat, and waited for the treat. The majority of the time, nothing came out!

What a blessing it is to be a behaviorist dog trainer. After all the training was completed, I was invited to the church rectory for lunch. I will never forget Father Davies ringing a small silver bell to have lunch served.

Sometime during the training lessons, I mentioned to Father Lanning that I thought the wine used for communion was the best ever. Well, my departing gift was a bottle of red wine that is normally given for communion; a great, unique dog training experience; fun times; lunch at the church rectory; a bottle of wine; and a tearful goodbye.

This was quite an endeavor in my forty years of dog training, and I feel blessed to have met and helped Father Davies and Father Lanning. God bless!

Training notes:

In this case, the focal point was on controlling the dogs when out for a walk. The heel command is the ideal means of control in order to prevent a dog from responding to distractions. A prudent dog owner should recognize this and persevere in teaching the heel command. A Seeing Eye dog would never knock anybody into a hedge when guiding his/her owner, except as a protective instinct due to provocation. Always remember to use discipline with love!

Buddy and Five Nuns

IN THE FALL of 1998, one of my few selected unique calls came from a school and residence home for troubled teenage girls. The caller was from the Mother Superior at the residence who informed me that if their newly acquired dog was not trained, the hierarchy would order Buddy, a Newfoundland, removed from the premises. Buddy happened to wander onto the school grounds, and one of the nuns allowed him into the building. Buddy became the school's mascot!

On arrival, I was greeted by a nun and escorted into a large room. The nun asked that I wait until more of the sisters were present for my presentation. I placed my attaché case onto a long table and patiently waited for them to arrive. I sat there, thinking that this particular training event would only come once in a lifetime. After all, how many dog trainers have an opportunity to train a dog owned by five nuns?

Followed by a long wait, the sisters entered the room. As usual, I proceeded to explain what my dog training program was all about and then asked to see Buddy. A nun named Evelyn went down the hall to retrieve the dog out of his cage. Buddy, a large Newfoundland, was escorted in by Sister Evelyn, I knew at once that this wouldn't be easy training, especially when Mother Superior mentioned that Buddy had been showing signs of dominance with a selected number of the nuns, a male dog included in a pack with five females! This was going to take a concentrated approach when teaching my dog training method to five nuns that previously cared for Buddy while employing endless love!

Sister Corrine signed the contract, and the lessons were started. I asked for two volunteers to learn the training to avoid the dog from being confused. Allowing too many people attempting to learn the training at the same time would create a lack of consistency.

My appointments were scheduled at a time for me to have lunch with all the nuns in the cafeteria. Great food and interesting conversations before each training lesson became a once-in-a-lifetime gift.

The dog training seemed like it was progressing positively until that one particular day, when I was going to be late due to a thunderstorm in the area. When I finally arrived, I was told that one of the nuns was bitten by Buddy. She was the oldest and perhaps the one who was too overloving with Buddy.

This is how this unfortunate event unfolded: Buddy was outside to relieve himself, and when he came back into the building, he was greeted instantaneously with a towel flung over his head to dry him off. This quick motion, along with a blinding towel over Buddy's head, frightened him enough to bite. The Sister was bitten on her hand and arm. I just wish that my arrival had been earlier so that I could have prevented this tragedy from happening.

Mother Superior ordered me to place Buddy into the school's van and remove the dog from the premises. I drove Buddy to my kennel then returned the SUV to the school residence.

I felt bad about this happening and wish I had the opportunity to finish the training program. Buddy's behavior needed to be desensitized by using discipline with love!

Sister Evelyn engaged in a condition called "standing over," which was perceived by Buddy as a threat, therefore resulting in a defensive bite. A bit of professional advice: Never go over the top of a dog's head when hugging, petting, applying a collar or the use of any forcible seizure—example: a sudden movement when throwing a towel over a dog's head!

Remember, dogs are genetically programmed for survival! Taking the time to study and understand these genetics will give you the advantage for positive results when training your dog. During the near completion of Buddy's training, the majority of people would find it hard to believe that this loving dog had ever bitten anyone. I can't stress enough that you have the responsibility to understand that your dog is just being a dog. Anthropomorphism is the reason why the majority of dog owners fail to train their best friend correctly!

He was a large male dog among five small women, who never represented pack leadership over Buddy. Male dogs generally will obey a male quicker than a female. In a dog pack, it is usually a male that is the pack leader; however, using my method, a female can become leader over her dog and perhaps never worry about being bitten.

Programming the correction "no" within the structure of the dog training lessons is essential in order to gain respect from your dog.

Finally, discipline with love, there isn't any better method.

Marne and Jax

DOG TRAINING FOR the disabled requires a unique specialized method. It demands a skilled, educated trainer, who clearly understands what is required to accommodate the specific needs of a disabled individual. The essentials needed are a dog willing to please, a determined family member helping the disabled person, and most of all, the disabled dog owner having strong motivation to help complete a positive outcome.

One day, I received a phone call from Marne, who was in a wheelchair, and needed her dog to perform certain tasks that she was unable to perform on her own.

My first response was that I didn't do this type of specialty dog training that her dog may never qualify, and therefore she may have to look into purchasing a dog trained for her specific needs.

She told me that she had spoken to other dog trainers, who told her that her dog, Jax, could not be trained for this type of assistance. All the trainers she spoke with agreed that she needed to purchase a specialty companion dog. She was adamant that she loved Jax and would never replace him to purchase another dog. Besides, a companion dog would cost much more that she could afford to pay. She continued to reply by mentioning that not one of the dog trainers was willing to attempt helping her to train Jax. In a soft tone, she said, "You are my last hope!"

I agreed to come over and evaluate Jax and determine if he could be trained to be a companion dog. Obviously, I knew this was a special situation that challenged my skills; however, it also touched my heart.

When I arrived for the consultation, I had no idea what to expect. The majority of my lessons are quite similar as far as behavioral problems are concerned, therefore always knowing what to expect. Marne's case was like no other! Meeting Marne was quite an experience for me. Here was a young lady in a wheelchair, who was only able to use the upper half of her body. After meeting with this courageous woman, there was no doubt in my mind that this was my calling to train Jax in assisting Marne.

Marne's mother, Mickey, said that I needed a new challenge in dog training. At the time, I needed all the support available in order to take on this endeavor. I was even further encouraged when Mickey informed me that she is a teacher for disabled children and had experience in psychology. Marne's mother would later prove to be the reason why I was successful in fulfilling the most challenging adventure of my professional dog training career.

When I entered her house, Jax, a black male Labrador, came bounding toward me, jumping up, and was totally out of control. Jax was only eight months old, undisciplined, and wouldn't come when called. The recall was especially difficult when Jax was outside in the backyard. Jax, like many dogs who are left outside in the backyard unsupervised, considered the yard his domain. It was his place to run, bark, urinate, dig, and chew. And without supervision, he had a conditioned behavior that is difficult to break.

Mickey was right when she said I needed a new challenge, and perhaps, unknowingly, a divine intervention was solidly taking place. This was going to take much more than my prior experience afforded me. Jax was an eight-month-old hyperactive Labrador retriever, absent of any foundation training, possessive of anything retrieved, and refused to come when called, which I knew right away would have to be his first and most essential lesson.

I began, in earnest, researching the training used with hunting dogs with the main focus on teaching Jax to retrieve things for Marne. Jax had to be taught to hold an item, retrieve it, bring it back on recall, and release it. I ordered training dummies used to train Labradors to retrieve in hunting. I also purchased a wild animal scent to apply to the dummies as a scented dummy would encourage Jax to be more interested in picking up the dummy, holding it, and eventually releasing it. Releasing the dummy would prove instrumental toward the success of this training. Jax would have to pick up items Marne dropped and place them into her lap. I was determined to succeed in teaching this to Jax.

Teaching Jax to heel also became a must if he was to walk on the left side of Marne's wheelchair and avoid him from ever pulling Marne while she is in the chair! Heel conditions the dog to join up with you, which in turn facilitates the "come when called" command in which I was determined to accomplish!

Once Jax started coming on command, it was time to teach him to retrieve the dummy and release it on command. An audacious, young, high-energy Labrador was becoming the companion dog that Marne earnestly required. My off-leash control method became instrumental for Marne, who would be in a wheelchair for the rest of her life. After several weeks, Jax listened on and off the leash.

A week after the training was completed, I received an urgent phone call from Marne's mother. She told me Jax was doing great, but when they went to the shopping mall, he bolted through the mall door, upsetting Marne. After calming Mickey down, I assured her that this would never happen again.

I set up a time to meet Marne, Jax, and Mickey at the mall. I made sure I was there a few minutes before Marne arrived. The entrance was two sets of entrance doors. Jax was cooperative going through the first set of doors. The problem was the second door, which entered into the mall, where Jax began to bolt.

Dogs react to the environment they are presently in. Jax had never been exposed to mall commotion, and the movement of so many people excited him!

When I saw Max bolt through the second door, I ran out from behind my hiding place, grabbed the leash, and corrected him, then I proceeded to work with him on the sit-stay command several times while the door was opened and closed. I didn't leave until he stopped pulling Marne through the doorway. The humorous side of the story, according to Marne's mom, was that thereafter, Jax would always look for me after entering the second set of doors.

One thing that must be kept in mind is that a companion or Seeing Eye dog must be conditioned to obey while exposed to every conceivable condition.

I witnessed a similar training procedure while sitting in my car outside a veterinary hospital. A Seeing Eye instructor and trainee were working a German shepherd on the corner adjacent to me. The dog attempted to cross the street before stopping to check for danger. The instructor quickly ran over, grabbed the short traffic lead, and gave a strong collar correction. The dog was brought back to the curb until he performed correctly. The case in point is that discipline is necessary to have the desired control expected from your dog.

Jax, the companion dog, and the German shepherd Seeing Eye dog are trained to guide and support disabled people. Therefore, these trained dogs have to obey under all types of environmental conditions. This not only pertains to service dogs but all dogs in training. The proof of any training method is consistent positive results. I mention this only because there are three types of people: those who make things happen, those who watch things happen, and those who wondered what happened. In Marne's case, Mickey, Marne, and I made things happen. Those who criticize the leash-and-collar-correction method are still wondering what happened.

After the completion of the training, I asked Marne to call before she left for her home in California. We made an appointment to meet. When I entered the house, I was immediately impressed to see Jax in the down-stay position. The majority of dogs never stay in the down when I enter their home, especially with dogs I haven't seen in a while.

Marne asked me to sit on the couch. Jax didn't move until Marne gave him the release command "okay," and not until then did I receive a remarkable greeting from Jax. Marne dropped a computer disk onto the floor and ordered Jax to pick it up. Jax retrieved the disk, walked over to Marne, and placed the disk into her lap. I seldom get emotional, but this magical moment brought joyful tears to my eyes. I told Marne how inspirational, brave, and deeply admired she was. I then thanked Marne's mom, Mickey, for her devotion, love, and time she dedicated to the training program. Without her,

I truly believe that the training outcome would not have been as successful. This was the most memorable, touching, and rewarding experience of my forty-year dog training career!

Training notes:

First worth mentioning is that Jax was definitely too young for this type of training program. Perseverance, research, knowledge, commitment, and perhaps blessed with divine intervention all aided in my being able to deliver a positive ending. My first priority was to teach Jax the heel command. Experience taught me that if a dog learns to heel, it will be much easier to teach him to come when called. The heel command is also necessary for the control needed in order for all other commands to work more effectively.

The discipline/correction "no" is intensified by using the full-leash correction in the heel command. This is beneficial for dealing with the many distractions encountered out on the street, sidewalk, etc.

Jax had to respond every time to the "come when called" command in order for this specialized training to work. The use of a "throw chain" is beneficial in conditioning a positive response to this command. It's considered the pecking order for off-leash control. This method was crucial in order for Marne to have control while confined to a wheelchair.

At the shopping mall, the use of a prong collar became necessary to prevent Jax from bolting through a heavy door. He could have caused injury not only to Marne but other people surrounding her. The prong collar was attached to a two-foot tab. This is the same type of tab used by the Seeing Eye dog training instructor. I felt that a prong collar would help quicker than a chain training collar in order to control Jax. Marne was instructed to have the prong collar, with tab, placed onto Jax after going through the first set of doors to the mall entrance. The association with the use of the prong collar helped tremendously in preventing Jax from bolting through the door, leading to the main entrance to the mall. This gave Marne the necessary control to prevent Jax from pulling her wheelchair and was key in gaining control of Jax under distraction.

Research on hunting dog training, specifically retrieving and animal scent, was instrumental in encouraging Jax to retrieve. Next, I taught Jax to take and release the dummy. This was followed by dropping and throwing the dummy for Jax to retrieve and drop into Marne's lap. Eventually, Jax would retrieve any item Marne dropped and place the item onto her lap. Mission accomplished! God bless, Marne!

Sammy the Bichon (Saved by His Olfactory)

SAMMY THE BICHON was just over a year old during the time I trained him. His behavioral problems consisted of grabbing personal items, jumping up onto the family's children, begging at the table, going into the garbage, and eliminating in the house. He was also very disobedient! I explained to the dog's owners that when your best friend is over six months of age and still eliminates in the house, the behavior is considered an elimination behavioral problem. It is true that although it may fall under the housebreaking behavior, it is dealt with by using a different method to solve the problem.

Sammy's owner, the wife of a doctor, was the only family member participating in the training program. Like many women, she overindulged this cute little dog and did not discipline him. Love without any standard of discipline enhances the dog's opportunity for exhibiting authority over the owner. One standard form of this behavior is scent elimination in the house. Sammy elected to choose an area in a secretive and far-off corner of the living room. I thought this would be an easy behavior to break due to the fact that he was eliminating in only one specific area. My scent elimination method is effective and works 99 percent of the time, but bichons are known to be difficult to housebreak and even harder to break after six months of age.

I always compared myself to Peter Falk in the TV series *Colombo*. Colombo was a homicide detective who always calculated all evidence he came upon. With enough concentration and the will to solve a murder, he never failed! I was determined to break Sammy of his elimination behavioral problem using a method that always worked for me. When arriving the following week, I felt confident that Sammy was no longer eliminating in the living room. The episode to follow was a first in my long dog training career. The method seemed like it was progressing until my arrival on the follow up lesson. I noticed Sammy would approach me slowly, all the while keeping a safe distance away from me. This behavior is called flight distance, which is a buffer zone between the dog and any animal or human that he may feel insecure about. I noticed when Sammy approached, me his nostrils were working overtime, trying to get a good scent of me. After some serious hard sniffing, he realized it was truly Uncle Kurt, and he slowly backed away. Paula was out of the room at the time, but on her return, she quickly reminded me that my method failed. I then asked Paula for a clean rag or towel. I unbuttoned my shirt and wiped my body with the cloth. I instructed her to place this cloth where Sammy is eliminating.

On our next scheduled lesson the following week, I arrived through the side door to the kitchen and was greeted by Paula. On the kitchen table was a stack of cut terry cloths. Paula asked me to wipe them on my body so that they would all have my scent. The scented rags, when placed in Sammy's favorite elimination area, solved the behavioral problem.

In summary, if you become alpha by applying a concrete training program, your dog will positively respond to the corrections needed to solve the majority of behavioral problems. In Sammy's case, he had become conditioned to respect me, and my scent in the elimination area was enough to deter this behavior.

Training notes:

An elimination behavioral problem is one of the more difficult behaviors to correct. Usually, a dog will select one area of the house to eliminate in; however, a small percentage of dogs will select two or three areas. I can't emphasize enough how important it is to first obedience train your dog before trying to correct any behavioral problems. A dog has to be conditioned to the "no" correction before any attempt is made in trying to solve behavior problems.

The following method describes an easy method that can be used to correct an elimination behavior once the dog has been conditioned to the "no" correction:

First, squirt the elimination with bitter apple. Leash the dog and bring him over to the area and put his nose into the elimination, simultaneously giving the "no" correction, then thoroughly clean the area. Soak an ordinary clean dish sponge in water. Squeeze it until damp, and apply several squirts of bitter apple into the sponge. Place the sponge on a piece of cardboard in the area where your dog is eliminating, then reinforce the correction by bringing your dog over to the area and bring the sponge up to his nose and repeat the "no" correction. Keep the loaded sponge in the area, repeating the correction each day until your dog subsides from eliminating. *Be* sure you keep the sponge damp with bitter apple.

All dog owners can establish the alpha status. When instructed using my training method, discipline with love!

Toni Ann and Bruno

GERMAN SHEPHERDS HAVE always been a favorite breed of mine, and I owned four at the same time! The breed is wonderful to train and driven to please its owner. Once you establish dominance, commands will follow with ease—well, not all German shepherds, as I was soon to find out!

Bruno was high energy, young, and never had any puppy foundation training. Bruno did what Bruno wanted to do and could care less about pleasing any member of the family. Bruno's home consisted of four members with only two interested in the training program. When there are one or two family members that show little or no interest, you can bet; unquestionably, there will be a problem in having consistency within the dog training method. In this case, it was the father who chose to stay out of the lessons. His remark was, "Bruno listens to me. Just teach the wife and daughter, Toni Ann!" That indicated to me that he had no respect for me or the training method.

This will be a major obstacle, only because I formally believe that humans should also show respect for their dog; after all, I believe that dogs are family members! Understanding German shepherds helped me to gain positive control when using the collar-and-leash training. After the completion of leash training, I prepared the owner and dog for off-leash control. The method is first taught inside the home, where we have the advantage of controlled space. I sectioned off an area of the house in order to attain a positive "come" when called. A small area leaves few options for the dog to run off to a secure area to avoid the come-when-called command. Bruno seemed to be doing well with the mother and daughter. Up to this point, all seemed positive until the husband told me, "I'm spending money on commands he listened to before you trained him!" Insults never mixed well with me, and I knew I had to show tenacity toward getting this dog trained. Anyway, I knew by this time that the dog was Toni Anne's, and knowing this gave me the incentive to hang in there for the young thirteen-year-old girl! The drama unfolded during the off-leash control method while in the backyard. Bruno had other ideas, none of which connected with me teaching him to come when called.

I was about to learn a significant fault in my presentation with "come" when a dog is oblivious to commands while in their backyard, especially this dog—a high energy, adolescent German shepherd boy! My off-leash control method has a success rate of 90 percent. Bruno truly qualified for the remaining 10 percent. In the yard, he just wanted to run around and play ball and was not inspired to listen to any commands! But why? What happened? I was left wondering and troubled by the fact that I could not easily gain off-leash control with Bruno. There had to be a reason why Bruno refused to listen to my commands while in his backyard. Here I was, halfway through my dog training career, and the method seemed to be failing me. I trained countless number of dogs, including German shepherds, to respond to my off-leash control method outside. The majority of these lessons were performed in the backyard of the client's home. All outside off-leash lessons were firmly taught only with fenced-in or tightly enclosed areas. The following questions were essential in order to understand why Bruno refused to come when called.

I needed to know, when Bruno was a puppy, was he always let out to eliminate by himself, or did any family members go outside with him? It's important that when teaching housebreaking, a family member went out into the yard with Bruno, also what their interactions were like during the time spent with him. I asked if Bruno was allowed out on his own and for how long a period of time was he left outside in the yard.

I also asked if, as Bruno grew older, any family member went out into the yard to play with him, and if so, was it fetching ball, rough play (tug toy), or was Bruno just playing keep-away?

Bruno was unsupervised when left in the backyard, allowing him to dominate the yard, which is the reason why he was so hard to control when I attempted the come-when-called off-leash lesson.

I didn't want to disappoint Toni Ann and was determined to have Bruno respond positively to her commands off leash in the backyard.

Training notes:

The number one rule in dog training when losing control off leash is to attach the leash back onto the dog's training collar. This will always enable the trainer to regain enough control over the dog to implement behavior modification by using positive reinforcement. Remember, the neck is the center of control! Only when you have enough confidence and are satisfied with the dog's response with leash control is it time to teach the off-leash control method. Your dog should always come (off leash) when called!

Remember, when your dog is allowed into the yard unsupervised, he will eventually get conditioned to control this area of the property, which can result in digging holes; running the fence; barking; eating plants and grass; chewing young trees, summer furniture, and wood decks. The truth is, he is just being a dog, doing natural doggie antics.

It's imperative for a responsible dog owner to go outside with their puppy when teaching the housebreaking program. This is always performed on a leash. A leash gives you the advantage of conditioning your puppy to eliminate in a selected area. After the puppy eliminates, call him/her and offer a treat for the good behavior. The positive outcome is twofold: eliminating outside and coming when called.

Once the come command is controlled, and the sit command in attained, always have the puppy sit in front of you on recall. This conditions him to obey you when outdoors.

Remember, sit is the first position in submission! You will notice this when his paw is raised slightly off the ground when sitting. Remember also that playtime is only after training and is an advantageous association with training.

Foundation training provides early conditioning in communication with your puppy using the sit, stay, down, come, heel commands and the corrective "no." This will help your young adult dog respond appropriately when distracted.

A well-trained dog is one that you can always control during the three S distractions: sight, sound, and scent. Always remember, discipline with love!

Out of Control Rottweiler

MANY DOG-HUMAN RELATIONSHIPS are connected to cultural ideas that have been handed down from generation to generation. Facts in human-dog relationships have been substantially tied to the truth. However, many of these facts are not reliable when communicating with your dog. What Grandfather felt was the only way to train a dog may not apply to our modern-day ways.

This dog story is one full of love, respect within a family, and with a positive outcome.

On arrival for my consultation, I was greeted by a lovely couple with five sons, a rottweiler, and a white dove. The dove, to me, was extremely inspirational.

I was told that Rotti Boy was usually tied up outside and only one of the sons could handle him without fear of being bitten. Currently tied up and left outside for a long period of time is detrimental to any dog's behavior. In this particular situation, Rotti Boy was tied up outside and kept away from the family (pack) for a lengthy time period. Being alone and tied up caused the dog to become extremely frustrated and caused severe anxiety, which in turn caused him to redirect his frustration into aggression. This form of aggression is more prevalent in certain breeds of dogs, like the rottweiler. Any person that the dog is unfamiliar with may be subject to being bitten when approached, even if the intention is to befriend him. All it takes is misjudgment on the length of the lead that the dog is tied too.

During my initial phone conversation with Rotti Boy's owner, I was informed that he showed aggression toward some members of the family. The aggression presented itself when other family members attempted to untie him. James, the sixteen-year-old, was the only one able to untie Rotti Boy without fearing a bite. Anyone else within striking distance could end up being jumped upon and bitten.

During my initial consultation, I instructed James to go into the backyard and leash up the dog and bring him out in the front of the house, where I could safely evaluate him. There was only a corral-type fence that separated me from James and his dog. I firmly instructed James to stay on the lawn and to keep Rotti Boy a safe distance from me. The plan was for me to instruct James on how to apply the training collar and leash and then safely transition the leash to me. While I was instructing him, James allowed the dog to pull toward the corral fence, and Rotti Boy was then able to squeeze half his body under it. This close call could have resulted in a bite if it wasn't for my quick reflexes.

Following my instructions, James rechecked the training collar to assure it was on correctly and then checked to be sure that the training leash was correctly hooked onto the collar. He then proceeded with the dog from the grass onto the street, keeping the dog on his right side using only a few feet of slack with the leash. I then instructed him to keep his dog close to him while he handed me the training leash so that Rotti Boy was securely on my left side. We proceeded to walk with the dog, while I executed a few corrective jerks with the leash. This was a significant procedure in order for me to see how Rotti Boy would react to my authority. I instructed James to let go of his leash and stand by it as I further evaluated the dog.

The evaluation proved successful, and I had full confidence that Rotti Boy would gradually evolve into a well-trained, trusted dog!

All the family members participated in the training sessions, were very attentive, and followed my dog training instructions.

Training notes:

Never ever tie up a dog for a long period of time. This could cause anxiety, frustration, loneliness, boredom, and stress, which could cause aggression in your dog.

My intention is always to educate my clients on human-dog relationships. Keeping a dog tied up outside is a cultural enigma in our society. I truly feel, if there is something that is detrimental to a dog, it is my obligation to inform and explain to those participating in my dog-training program how that adversity could psychologically impact him. Certain traditions handed down from generation to generation are held steadfast by families. In this case, the father had grown up with the family dog tied up outside. This occasion, a mixed-up rotti had to be untied, socialized, trained, and become a loving family member. Even though he showed some early aggression, he soon would develop into a loving dog.

By the third week of training, Rotti Boy was playing with me on the living room floor. And when I was on my back, he playfully licked my face. Looking up, I couldn't help but notice the white dove witnessing the success of discipline with love!

Bumper (and the Unintentional Bump)

YOU MAY FIND this story a coincidence, humorous, or violent. Then again, like me, I found it to be all three experiences simultaneously.

It was in early fall when I experienced this unique drama. On this particular day, I was scheduled to go on a consultation and hopefully sign up a client for dog obedience communication.

As I approached the client's home, I noticed that there was little or no room to park my van. I gradually pulled up toward the neighboring house, which had one car parked in front of it. I carefully tried to angle the van in front of the parked car while trying not to land on their lawn. In this area, the lawns meet the street, minus curbs. At the last second, I turned to my left to prevent parking on the lawn, forgetting that the right end of my bumper was slightly angled. A relieved feeling of having prevented parking on the lawn soon turned into a sick feeling of anxiety! My bent-out bumper hooked the front bumper of the parked car and consequently pulled the car's bumper halfway off.

A woman soon appeared at the front door of the house, and in a panicked voice she yelled, "What happened to my car?"

I was trying in my humble way to be both sympathetic and concerned at the same time. I replied, saying, "I'm sorry, ma'am, but I somehow hooked your bumper."

She said, "My husband is going to be extremely upset!"

The husband, a stocky man, came out from the backyard, shouting, "What happened?"

His wife related the sad news to him, and he came charging towards me, yelling, "I'm going to kick your ass!"

I quickly removed my jacket and then shifted into a defensive stance. My pugilist experience in the US Navy was about to be applied; therefore I was ready to defend myself. When this raging bull of a husband neared within ten feet of me, his wife grabbed him from behind. She then yelled for her friends, who were walking down the block about fifty yards away. They quickly ran back to help her restrain the raging husband.

The shouting and name-calling summoned a neighbor to leave his party and cross the street. He asked me if I wanted him to beat up the husband. I quickly said no to this guy, who showed signs that he was intoxicated! Next, the police showed up. What a circus! The friend wasn't of much help and added more insulting words: "You are lucky my friend's wife is holding him, or he would have beaten you up!" Of course I was thinking that if he really wanted to beat me up, his wife wouldn't have been strong enough to hold him back. At any rate, I was relieved that physical contact was avoided!

I humbly explained that the car would be fixed and paid for. They owned a dog, and as always, a magical connection transcended for all to see what I really am about. This couple, who only fifteen minutes ago wanted to attack me, were now inviting me into their house. All of us seemed much calmer and were able to work out the details on how to proceed on repair and payment. It so happened that they had a friend who owned a body shop, and the plan was to go there after I did my consultation.

I composed myself after this traumatic episode and finally arrived next door for the consultation with a young couple. They owned a Labrador retriever with the typical behavioral problems associated with this breed. After evaluating the dog, I then proceeded to fill out the dog training contract.

When I asked my client what the name of his dog is, he replied, "Bumper!"

I replied, "Are you kidding me?"

Baffled by my response, I quickly explained what had taken place prior to the appointment. My client responded by saying that he hated this neighbor, and if he had witnessed the commotion, he would have been glad to have beaten the guy up! Of course, I was relieved that this aggression never happened.

Soon after, I left their home and, once outside, reflected on the recent event. I laughed to myself; after all, how could I be upset over a bumper? Really now, let's face it, I'd be connecting for six weeks with a wonderful dog, whose name was Bumper!

Training notes:

Bumper ended up a well-trained dog. Labradors are high energy and prove challenging the first couple of lessons.

Knowing the breed type is a major component when training any dog. Insight, experience, and natural ability will all result in a more positive outcome.

If you develop a confident and professional demeanor, even when threatened, the reward will be a reflection of discipline with love! It has been said, discretion is the better part of valor! I will always smile when hearing the name Bumper.

Aggressive Sam (the Black Labrador Retriever)

I WAS RECOMMENDED to Sam's owner by her veterinarian. She called me to evaluate Sam, who was exhibiting aggressive behavior. Sam was a three-year-old Labrador with tremendous size and strength.

During the first few lessons in the home, Sam never showed aggression. Later, I received a hysterical phone call from Sam's owner, saying that Sam showed his teeth and snapped at her when she tried to pull him off the couch! She said, "You have to do something, or else he goes!" I immediately made the decision to come and pick Sam up and take him to my training kennel.

After a couple of days of training, I hadn't experienced any aggression with Sam. He loved his obedience lessons and always looked forward to playing ball with me after the training. I decided to try an exercise used in attack training to see if Sam showed any form of aggression.

I raised an old broom handle stick over Sam's head, and he snapped it in half, so I knew that someone in Sam's environment had to be showing anger toward him, which triggered his aggression.

I called Sam's owner and suggested that the training should resume in the home with both her and her maid.

When I arrived with Sam, his owner wasn't present, and in her place was the housemaid. This was my first meeting with the maid. She offered me coffee, and after a few minutes of cordial conversation, I asked if she ever experienced aggressive behavior with Sam. Her response was, "When Sam won't listen to me, I take a mop handle and chase him into the bathroom and close the door so he will be out of my way!" She also said, "I have no problem after cracking him over the head, so he listens to me!"

She wasn't the owner, and she never participated in any of the training lessons; therefore, later that day, I phoned Sam's owner and told her what the maid told me. I explained that the maid's actions were the reason for Sam's aggression and suggested she speak with her, but she quickly responded, saying, "She is family, and the dog has to go!" The client was not interested in having me work with her or her maid to solve the problem and was not open to any behavioral training or suggestions. She abruptly hung up the phone.

It is unfortunate that some people are so unwilling in understanding their pet dog. Sam would have been a fine house dog if it weren't for what I call the villain, an outsider who has no positive relationship with the family dog.

These people usually break the consistency of the training method and disrupt the dog from being trained. They could be friends of family, people living or renting, dog walkers, relatives, neighbors, or house cleaners.

If Sam's owner had agreed to have her housemaid participate in the training and if the housemaid was willing to participate, the aggressive behavior problem most likely would never have occurred.

Unfortunately, employees are trained and hired to do specific chores relating to the home, and 99 percent will fail to follow any instructions relating to a dog training program. They never anticipated this duty when applying for the job.

Training notes:

If a dog owner hires a person to live in the home, then that person needs to participate in the training of the dog. Household members who do not participate in the dog training program will give inconsistent commands to your dog. Consistency is supportive in order for the training method to be a success. Dog sitters should also communicate properly in accordance with the training method.

Common behaviors used by untrained dog owners: moving abruptly toward the dog, pulling or shoving the dog, or raising items over the dog's head with intent to hurt. This threat is referred to as standing over. In canine body language, standing over is received as a threat and will elicit a fight-or-flight response.

Remember, a well-trained dog will never show aggression when you stand over him! Discipline with love conditions the dog to trust you!

Duke (the Bernese Mountain Dog)

EARLY IN MY dog training career, I bred and trained German shepherds. My personal experience training shepherd puppies allowed me the opportunity to better communicate more efficiently during their critical period, six to sixteen weeks of age. This early puppy communication was indispensable, therefore allowing me to become better qualified when training future puppies during my professional dog training career.

As a rule, I trained the majority of puppies in their home. Early association and socialization with other dogs are essential for raising a well-rounded young dog. That being the case, I would train selected puppies at my home, socializing them with my dogs.

Duke the puppy was a joy to meet. His expressive exuberance, consisting of yelping happiness, touched my heart immediately. It is of extreme significance to train a puppy correctly in order to later on have a well-trained adult dog. I started puppy training Duke in his home environment. His pack consisted of two adults, three children, and a rabbit. The consultation further allowed me a concrete evaluation to apply my educated puppy knowledge. This concentrated effort was essential. The pack leader of the family is a famous TV celebrity!

When the family vacationed, I would take Duke to stay with me and my two adult Doberman pinschers, Autumn (male) and Shade (female). My earlier experience with puppy and adult socialization training was quickly put to the test. Duke's antics in his home environment consisted of one major behavioral problem: undisciplined rough playing with three children!

Interacting with two adult-grown Dobermans gave Duke a quick introduction in pack discipline. Communication between adult dogs and puppies is interesting to watch. Duke's communication with my two adult Dobermans was a joy to witness. My two dogs were excellent with Duke. All three played under my supervision. Duke's rough play of jumping and nipping was soon corrected by Autumn and Shade. After this quick introduction to the pecking order, Duke soon learned to play a submissive role. Early associations with other dogs, like my own, is essential for developing a well-rounded young dog. In this case, it conditioned Duke to interact with the children and other household pets without any incidence of aggression. Occasionally, play would get somewhat rough, but Duke quickly learned his place and became submissive when necessary.

This communication helped me to more clearly understand the temperament of a Bernese mountain dog. I witnessed the amount of time during fight play that it took Duke to express nonthreatening aggression; after all, any puppy would react with some aggression when two full-grown adult dogs are roughhousing with him.

On one occasion, Duke was left with me on a snowy winter day. All three dogs played happily as the snow accumulated on their coats. Duke, having the longest coat, ran around, looking like a little snowman. It was a joy to watch!

Duke received a combination of training at and away from his home. Today, Duke is coexisting with a loving family of three children, two adults, and one rabbit. Duke is one of many outstanding dogs who learned discipline with love!

Training notes:

The pecking order is an innate communication used with a pack of dogs. Higher ranking members of the pack keep order by nipping and growling. This keeps the pack cohesive and allowing a longer survival.

It was truly advantageous to have Duke in my company for obedience training. Puppy into adult communication training helped me to more clearly understand the Bernese mountain dog. I was able to condition Duke early to the discipline correction "no." This correction was only used as a last resort during rough play interaction with my two Dobermans. Furthermore, this training proved that discipline is the number one objective in controlling all dogs. If applied with understanding and knowledge, it will help all dog owners to feel totally secure with their best friend.

Remember, if you train your puppy, it will condition him to learn what you want him to learn, not what he wants to learn on his own! A trained dog is a man and woman's best friend when using discipline with love!

Max (and the Neighborhood Bully)

DURING EACH CONSULTATION, I carefully study the puppy or dog I'm asked to train. I will ask the owner if the dog was rescued, bought, and if so, where. I also ask whether the dog has been neutered or spayed, if there are any existing health problems, preexisting psychological problems from previous environment, socialization problems, pretraining, signs of aggression, or any other unfamiliar existing alien traits.

Max, a male German shepherd, was less than six months of age and full of energy (high powered) when I first evaluated him. This is a common trait among Shepherd breeds, especially if the dog comes from a breeder who breeds for protection. Max was bred in Europe, where Schutzhund training is prevalent. This training and breeding focus on obedience, tracking, agility, and attack.

I didn't see any signs of aggression in Max during the first few weeks of training. Max's owner then complained that he showed aggression toward a neighborhood dog a few blocks from his home. On the following lesson, Max; Jim, his owner; and I went for a walk toward the area where Max became aggressive.

The residential area consisted of homes on large parcels of property. The home in front of which Max was showing aggression had a dog contained by an invisible electric fence. When we were within fifteen feet of the property, this dog came charging toward the street, barking, growling, and baring his teeth! It was only normal for Max to become undiscriminating while propelling him into aggressive behavior. If Max could talk, he would say, "It's what I do!"

The dog may have been contained with the use of the invisible fence, although Max had no idea of this. Max was threatened by this bully charging at him, and he was ready to protect himself, along with his owner. Keep in mind, a dog's territorial instincts are strong and demanding. I proceeded training Max in this aggressive situation, eventually hoping to control his response while in a protective mode.

I advised Jim not to walk too close to the property where the dog was located and to stay a reasonable distance away, whereby Max could more easily pay attention to the training commands. We worked him in obedience training while gradually shortening the distance between Max and the property.

Jim called later on in the week to inform me that Max got into a fight with the dog living at the problem property. On this particular day, children were playing on the property with their dog. When the bully saw Max coming too close to his property, he charged toward Max. His pack members, being the family children, had to be protected, and therefore, his forward charge propelled him right through the electrically charged invisible fence and into a fight with Max.

This occurrence made desensitizing Max more difficult, and we began training him at a safe distance from any open property containing dogs. Max was doing great in obedience and was starting to heel well with distractions until a neighborhood dog was let out of a car unleashed. We were across the street when this dog, barking and growling, came charging aggressively, like a freight train, toward Max and me. All of a sudden, this aggressive dog darted to my left, and I quickly pulled Max toward my right. Max quickly reacted to protect me and dashed around my back, causing me to fall onto the street pavement while I was still holding onto the leash in desperation.

The charging dog was soon grabbed and controlled by his owner as I laid on the ground, bleeding from a scraped knee. Aggressive tunnel vision triggers a tremendous amount of strength in dogs, especially this type of German shepherd juiced with high energy. Max is truly a wonderful family dog. He enjoys playing soccer with Jim's children and other kids in the neighborhood. He has never intentionally attacked or bitten anyone.

Training notes:

An enclosed dog may break through the shock field if provoked while guarding property and family members.

Distractions, such as people passing, a bike rider, a mother pushing a baby carriage, children running and playing, or someone walking a dog could, at some point, excite a dog to break through the electric barrier.

Dog snatchers have an easy access to come unto the property, take off the collar, and steal your precious pet.

Rather than using an electric fence, I suggest a real fence to keep your loving dog safe. Free, roaming dogs may enter the property, leading to unwanted mating, disease, parasites, and aggressive acts.

Moreover, never leave your dog off the leash in any public area. Even a well-trained dog off leash may be difficult to control if sufficiently provoked. I personally don't approve of electric fence containments.

Romulus (Black Shepherd Boy)

DURING MY CAREER, I did a few breeding's using my German shepherds. My black bitch had only two pups, born black. I named them Romulus and Remus. I sold Remus, the female, to a wonderful family. I kept Romulus as my own personal dog. Housebreaking this puppy was a nightmare! Romulus would eliminate in his cage where he slept. Prior to Romulus, I encountered this behavior with a few of my clients and presented a diversified housebreaking program to deal with the problem. This was a difficult behavioral problem, but I was determined to solve it. I set my alarm for 2:00 a.m. to check on him and found that he hadn't eliminated. Each day that followed, I increased fifteen minutes until finally I was able to get up at my regular time to take Romulus out to relieve himself. He had a few more mishaps until he was six months old. This is one of the more difficult elimination behavioral problems to correct. Now I realized what my clients went through because now I personally experienced this behavioral problem.

The reward of this method was twofold; I solved the problem with Romulus and was now able to help future dog owners with elimination behavior issues.

Romulus was a sweet-natured shepherd, who I decided to use as a therapy dog and visit patients in the geriatric ward of a local hospital. Although some were reluctant to pet him because of his size and pure black color, the majority of patients loved him. By being socialized, this humanitarian service also helped Romulus to develop a positive sweet nature. Romulus served as a loving ambassador during his many visits to the hospital.

Soon after, I received a phone call from a previous client. She called to tell me that her shepherd died. She wanted desperately to replace him, and I knew Romulus would be the perfect dog for her. She was a young woman, lived alone, a real animal person. I sold Romulus to this woman and knew that he would have a long loving life with her. He not only shared his love with many patients in the hospital but most of all with his new owner.

Training notes (elimination behavioral problem):

Romulus was difficult to housebreak and therefore created an elimination behavioral problem. Working out a method on my own later helped many of my clients who owned a dog with the same behavior problem.

Zeus (Three-Year-Old Male Doberman)

ZEUS'S OWNER KEPT in touch with me ever since his Doberman pup arrived. I started the puppy training at ten weeks of age. When he turned six months old, I proceeded to teach the adult advanced-obedience program. Zeus had a sweet temperament and was a great student as long as the training method remained consistent. I say this only because, at times, there were inconsistencies in handling him by friends, neighbors, and visitors.

One day, a neighbor came over to play with Zeus. His rough play caused Zeus to be slightly injured. Zeus's owners checked him to be sure he wasn't seriously injured and then instructed him to go to place, which Zeus obediently did. In this case, "place" was his cage in a designated area in the house. This neighbor followed Zeus to his cage to make up with him. He reached over the top of the dog in his cage and consequently received a bite on the hand.

I met with Zeus's owners and explained why they should not have allowed the neighbor to follow Zeus to pet him in his cage.

Zeus was a well-trained Doberman, and there were never any other biting problems, a fortunate Dobie boy, loved by all.

Training notes:

This event gives me the opportunity to remind all dog owners of one ultimate consequence related to dog bites. Sadly, millions of dogs are euthanized every year in this country, all due to the fact that we humans have failed to communicate and provide a consistent atmosphere.

Anytime you go over the top of a dog, he may receive this gesture as a threat, especially if the dog does not know you well. The terminology for this behavior is called standing over. Dogs use this body language to show dominance over one another. For example, a dominant dog may put his paw or head over a lower-ranking dog to secure his dominance.

All negative behaviors are unacceptable, especially aggressive behavior. Therefore, it is imperative that a dog owner obedience train their dogs. This is the only way that you, as a dog owner, will set in motion a gateway to dog communication and truly understand how your dog reacts to your commands.

A dog owner is in charge of their dog, and all other individuals should respect this. When in doubt, place your dog in a secure area, away from whoever you want him away from. Be prudent with no regrets! All things considered, why not just train your dog using discipline with love.

Oliver (Motivating a Lazy Mastiff)

THIS DOG TRAINING story is short with a very interesting ending. I started training Oliver at the age of six months in his home for a doctor friend and his wife.

It was a warm summer day, the kind of weather I look forward to for outside training. Once Oliver was fitted with a training collar, I attached the leash and proceeded to walk him outside Oliver's designated training lesson, which would be heel on leash.

This wasn't the understanding Oliver had circling around in his head. Once we were well onto the lawn, Oliver selected a cool spot and laid down flat on his side. I exhausted all commands, bribes, voice sounds, and leash control, all to no avail! What was I to do? Oliver lay in the grass, refusing to budge all of his 150 lb.! As time appeared to stand still, I began wondering why my twenty-five years as a professional dog trainer was failing me. Proof that psychology is only available to the few who are serendipitously gifted, there will always be that one dog that proves difficult to train. What I'm really trying to say is, I could have trained half a dozen mastiffs before Oliver and not have this negative response!" Serendipity was soon to become my alliance.

It was time for me to come up with an innovation that would give me positive results. I lied down next to Oliver and began rubbing his belly while whispering sweet words to him. After assuring Oliver that all was wonderful in doggie land, I proceeded to execute my brainstorm. With a swift motion, I suddenly jumped up and said, "Come on, Oliver, let's play!" Oliver quickly jumped up on all four paws and gleefully ran with me onto the street. Once in the street,

I transferred his forward motion into the heel command, a gifted ending, allowing successful training.

Training notes:

One thing I have learned through the years when teaching the heel is that it affords me instant control over the many dogs I have trained. The majority of the time, I allow the dog to sniff around awhile before I proceed to teach the heel command. This not only relaxes the dog, but it also gives him the opportunity to relieve himself, if necessary. In dedication of Dr. Robert Schwartz, who passed away 2014, he truly loved Oliver!

The Milberg's Black Lab

EARLY IN MY dog training career, confident in my ability, without having any conception of what was about to unfold, paving the way to this event, which, in 1972, happened at an upper middle-class neighborhood in Great Neck, Long Island. The dog ownership consisted of a family of four: mother, father, and two daughters. They were all the proud owners of a black male Labrador. The younger of the two daughters volunteered to learn the dog training method, which began with the lesson, heel-on-leash command. We started out this lesson at her house and later ended up going over to the village, where there would be more distractions. This change in area presented a perfect opportunity for the dog to be trained in adverse conditions.

The problem was, the dog training instructor was distracted by something across the street! Directly in front of me was my sixteen-year-old student, heeling with her Labrador. I was walking too close behind both of them and was totally oblivious of why I was there in the first place because I was stupidly distracted.

The lesson is called the about-face correction, which is applied when the dog is pulling on the leash. The method is put to use by releasing the middle of the leash when or if your dog attempts to pull you. When executing this correction, it's important to have a firm grip of the leash handle with both hands, therefore affording you the necessary leverage to execute the full leash corrective jerk. Imagine the dog pulling at the end of the leash and this young lady jerking back in the opposite direction to correct him. Any intelligent human who is familiar with this method would carefully make sure that they stayed safely behind a person, who was in the process of applying this correction. Certainly, one would reason that the instructor should have been the intelligent one. Yes, I received a tremendous force that clocked me on the chin, and down I went for the ten counts! The young girl and her dog landed on top of me while I lay dazed on the sidewalk. Lesson learned for a dog trainer: Pay attention. Be sure to conduct yourself professionally at all times and never be directly behind your students when teaching the heel command.

Training notes:

It may have seemed like a humorous dog training lesson, which could have turned out to be more tragic than funny. After that event, I instructed my clients to be more vigilant when teaching their dog the heel lesson. Be aware of your surroundings, and use emphatic judgments. Prevent injury to other people, dogs, dog owners, and yourself. Prevention may also keep you out of the courts; after all, none of us want to be sued for something we could have easily prevented.

Ryder (and the Models)

RYDER WAS A two-year-old male dalmatian, who I trained for a wonderful woman named Madeline. Those of us who know the breed will also know that at any given time, without warning, they can quickly shift into dalmatian land. There are many breeds of dogs that let you know when it's time to take a break during training. Dalmatians leave you with the sense that all is going well, and they are obeying you. Then out of nowhere, without warning, they become a dog—meaning, "I'm doing what dogs love to do without taking any commands from my human companion!" Keep this last statement in mind as I tell you the following dog story.

It was sometime in the summer of 1985 when I received a phone call from a modeling agent. She was interested in having a variety of breeds to pose alongside female models. The dogs had to be well trained, nonaggressive, and safe around people. She asked if I have access to the dogs needed for her modeling project. I told her that it was possible for me to call previous clients with dogs of various breeds and ask if they were interested in having their dog model. I first arranged an appointment with her to not only meet but also display my portfolio with pictures of dogs that I've trained in the past couple of years. The meeting was at a dance wear company, where the modeling would take place. She loved the dog pictures and quickly elected a variety of breeds she was interested in. I told her that I would contact the owners to see if they would be interested.

Within a week, I was able to gain access to the majority of the dogs that she selected. First, I wanted the owners to bring their dogs to the location to become familiar with the surroundings. This was a critical evaluation; after all, safety was first before any photo shoot could take place. The dogs were walked around the area and slowly introduced to some of the models that would be posing with them. Before I could secure any training with the models, reinforcement in obedience was exercised inside and outside the building; this way, I had enough confidence that any dog that I used would listen to me unconditionally.

Everything seemed to be going successfully until it was Ryder's turn to pose. He was placed in a group with three models. Two of the models were standing, while the third was posing in a stretched-out position. Ryder was sitting near one of the standing models, although not too far from the outstretched model. I gave Ryder a final sit-stay command to ensure that he wouldn't release his pose until I instructed him to. The three models and Ryder looked glamorous and ready for the photo shoot to take place. Then the unexpected happened. Ryder walked over to sniff the outstretched model. The startled young model fell forward onto the floor. One of the standing models looked straight at me, smiling. I looked back, shaking my head no! It was bad enough that Ryder embarrassed the model without me thinking it was funny. Although I had to admit that it wasn't easy to stop from laughing. I quickly apologized and reassured the young lady that it wouldn't happen again. I suggested that I should take Ryder outside and come back, and we could proceed with the photo; this way, all involved had time to settle down, regroup, and go back to the drawing board. Ryder listened very well. You would, too, after a quick reminder outside that reinforced discipline into his thick dalmatian head. Oh, by the way, Madeline was nowhere in sight. She told me later that she immediately left the premises to avoid embarrassment. Despite it all, Ryder went on to live another nine years, giving Madeline dalmatian love.

Training notes:

Whenever dogs are used for modeling or any other work involving photography, discipline is essential. This can only be established through the use of a professional dog training method. Teaching commands with the use of distractions is important to create stability—in the case of Ryder, sit-stay! The stay command is vital when dogs are used for modeling.

Testimonials

"Jax"

He is very happy since his training. Thanks for teaching him to be such a well-behaved dog.

—Marne G.

"Hans"

Thank you for teaching Mommy and Daddy to understand my behavior. I know they were a handful. I see a vast improvement in them already.

—Bill and Lynda H.

"Shamrock"

Shamrock and I would like to thank you, thank you, thank you! We are so thrilled that we can finally take walks together! I know she is going to miss you.

—Heather

"Rollie"

I want to thank you for your phone advice and for being a wonderful dog trainer.

—Sue and Al M.

"Taylor and Rena"

Thank you for all you have done. You have taught my mom and dad so much. We will always be good dogs for that.

—The Anastasios

"Molly"

Thank you so much for helping me be the best dog. You are a great teacher. My parents thank you also. I'm feeling much happier and definitely less bored. I'm sending you this picture so you don't forget how cute I am, and you don't forget one of your best students. I'll miss you (and so will my mom and dad.)

—Hilary and Bill B.

"Zachary"

Thank you for turning Zachary into a calmer, more obedient dog. I appreciate all your patience with both him and me.

—Karon

"Buster"

Here is a picture we took with our daughter, Kayla, with Buster in our last training lesson. Buster has been doing so great since we learned so much with the lessons. He is a well-behaved dog.

—Dave and Kara B.

"Ryder"

There may be times when you will be sorry about something you said, sorry that you stayed too late or sorry that you went so early, sorry that you won something or lost. But all your life, you'll never be sorry you were kind.

—Madeline C.

"Hund"

Hund is doing very well. I work with him every day, and it really shows. As I told you, this training has made it possible for us to enjoy this pup more than any other. Many thanks!

—Maude D.

"True"

Uncle Kurt has been helping me train my German shepherd, True, who understandably has some bad habits (barking, circling people for attention) after he was locked in a small bathroom and suffered abuse for the first four years of his life. It was amazing to watch the soft-voiced gentlemen connect with True from the first moment he walked into my home. Uncle Kurt pointed out that some of True's disruptive behaviors can actually be traced to his wolf ancestry. He explained the reason for True's excited circling. Uncle calls it "greet to eat." I noticed a difference in True right after the first lesson. I felt we were more deeply connected, and I noticed that True looks into my eyes with new understanding and happy expectation. When it comes to dog trainers, I know what I want and what I don't want— no pronged collars cutting into my dog's neck, no choking, and certainly no breaking of his spirit. I want the training to come from love and understanding. So for all of you, readers, who emailed, asking me to recommend a trainer, here's Uncle Kurt's contact information. And, readers, FYI, while Uncle Kurt is putting True through his paces, he is also spending plenty of time teaching me to train True and be a better pet parent.

—Sharon Hubbard, Neighbor Newspapers

About the Author

KURT THOMAS WOLFF is a professional behaviorist dog trainer. He began his career as a graduate of Captain Haggerty's School for Dogs, a renowned dog training school in New York in 1971. He has spent his career teaching dog owners and their dogs his unique method of communication and understanding using discipline with love.

Having studied and worked with both the canine in the wild and the behavioral characteristics of a wide span of domestic dog breeds, Kurt has a unique perspective in fostering loving coexistence between people, families, and their dogs.

Kurt offers training from initial adoption and housebreaking behavior issues through puppy and adult training and specializes in special needs training, off-leash training, and personal protection. He is recommended and respected by veterinarians and rehoming organizations for rescued abandoned dogs.